초등 영단어 850 따라쓰기

기획 : 와이앤엠 어학연구소

와이 앤 엠

차 례

초등 영단어 850 따라쓰기

1. 학생과 학용품

album
앨범, 사진첩
[ǽlbəm]

album   album   album

bag
가방, 봉지
[bǽg]

bag   bag   bag   bag

blackboard
칠판
[blǽkbɔːrd]

blackboard   blackboard

board
판자, 게시판
[bɔːrd]

board   board   board

album	[앨범]	Let's buy him a photo album.	그에게 사진첩(앨범)을 사주자.
bag	[백]	This is my schoolbag.	이건 제 책가방이예요.
blackboard	[블랙보-르드]	She is writing on the blackboard.	그녀는 칠판에 글을 쓰고 있다.
board	[보-르드]	What's this new board for?	이 새 게시판은 어디에 쓸 거죠?

book
책
[buk]

book book book book

camp
캠프
[kæmp]

camp camp camp camp

chalk
분필
[tʃɔːk]

chalk chalk chalk chalk

class
수업, 학급
[klæs]

class class class

classmate
동급생
[klǽsmèit]

classmate classmate

book	[북]	Mom is reading a book for me. 엄마가 저에게 책을 읽어주고 계세요.
camp	[캠프]	Let's go camping. 캠핑하러 가자.
chalk	[초어크]	Let's buy blackboard and chalk. 칠판과 분필을 삽시다.
class	[클래스]	It's time to finish the class. 수업을 끝낼 시간이예요.
classmate	[클래스메이트]	She is my classmate. 그녀는 같은 반 친구에요.

classroom 교실 [klǽsrùːm]	classroom classroom
computer 컴퓨터 [kəmpjúːtər]	computer computer 
crayon 크레용 [kréiən]	crayon crayon crayon
desk 책상 [desk]	desk desk desk desk
eraser 지우개 [iréisəvər]	eraser eraser eraser 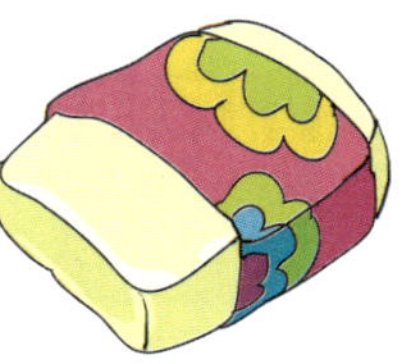

classroom [클래스루-ㅁ]	Don't jump in the classroom.	교실에서 뛰지 말아요.
computer [컴퓨-러ㄹ]	There are three compurters on the desk.	책상위에 컴퓨터가 3대 있어요.
crayon [크래이언]	I like to draw lines using crayons.	크래용으로 선긋는 것을 좋아해요.
desk [데스크]	There is a pencil on the desk.	책상 위에 연필 한 자루가 있어요.
eraser [이뢰이줘ㄹ]	Tom, can I borrow your eraser?	Tom, 지우개 좀 빌려줄래?

ink 잉크 [iŋk]	ink ink ink ink
learn 배우다 [ləːrn]	learn learn learn learn
lesson 수업 [lésn]	lesson lesson lesson
library 도서관 [láibreri]	library library library
math 수학 [mǽθ]	math math math math

ink	[잉크]	Uncle is filling the pen with ink.	삼촌이 펜에 잉크를 채워 넣고 계셔요.
learn	[러-ㄹ언]	I want to learn English.	전 영어를 배우고 싶어요.
lesson	[렛쓴]	I have no lesson today.	오늘은 수업이 하나도 없어요.
library	[라이브뢰뤼]	Mom and I often go to a library.	엄마랑 저는 가끔 도서관에 가요.
math	[매쓰]	Math is a very important subject.	수학은 매우 중요한 과목입니다.

8

middle school 중학교 [mídl skúːl]	middle school middle school
page 페이지, 쪽 [peidʒ]	page page page page
paper 종이 [péipər]	paper paper paper 
pen 펜 [pen]	pen pen pen pen pen
pencil 연필 [pénsəl]	pencil pencil pencil 

middle school	[미들 스쿨]	He is a middle school student.	그는 중학생입니다.
page	[페이쥐]	Open your page 6.	6쪽을 펴세요.
paper	[페이펄]	I need a sheet of paper.	종이 한 장이 필요하다.
pen	[펜]	Can I borrow your pen?	내가 네 펜을 빌릴 수 있을까? 혹은 펜좀 빌려줄래?
pencil	[펜쓸]	Do you have pencils?	너 연필 있니?

pin 핀 [pin]	pin pin pin pin pin pin
question 질문 [kwéstʃən]	question question
science 과학 [sáiəns]	science science science
school 학교, 수업 [skuːl]	school school school 
student 학생 [stjúːdənt]	student student student

pin	[핀]	Please, lend me a safety pin.	안전핀 좀 빌려 주시겠어요.
question	[퀘스천]	He put the question to me.	그는 나에게 그 질문을 했다.
science	[사이언스]	The science class was so boring.	과학 수업은 너무나 지루했다.
school	[스꾸-울]	After school, I came back home.	수업이 끝난 후, 나는 집으로 돌아 왔어요.
student	[학생]	How many students are there?	학생이 몇 명 있죠?

study
공부하다
[stʌ́di]

study study study study

table
테이블
[téibl]

table table table

teach
가르치다
[tiːtʃ]

teach teach teach

test
시험, 검사
[test]

test test test test test

vacation
방학
[veikéiʃən]

vacation vacation

study	[스떠디]	At school, I study English.	학교에서, 나는 영어를 공부한다.
table	[테이블]	There are two books on the table.	테이블 위에 책이 2권 있다.
teach	[티-취]	She teaches English at our school.	그녀는 학교에서 영어를 가르친다.
test	[테스트]	I had a test last Friday.	지난 금요일에 나는 시험을 봤다.
vacation	[베이케이션]	Summer vacation is finally over.	여름 방학이 드디어 끝이 났습니다.

2. 사람과 삶

aunt 아주머니, 이모 [ænt]	aunt aunt aunt aunt
baby 아기 [beibi]	baby baby baby baby
birthday 생일 [bə́ːrθdéi]	birthday birthday
boy 소년 [bɔi]	boy boy boy boy boy

aunt	[앤트]	I love my aunt Amy.	저는 Amy이모가 좋아요.
baby	[베이비]	The baby girl is my little sister.	그 여자 아기는 내 여동생이예요.
birthday	[벌쓰데이]	When is your birthday?	네 생일이 언제니?
boy	[보이]	Who is that boy?	저 소년은 누구니?

child
어린이
[tʃaild]

child   child   child   child

citizen
시민
[sítəzən]

citizen   citizen   citizen

course
진로, 과정
[kɔːrs]

course   course   course

friend
친구
[frend]

friend   friend   friend

girl
소녀
[gəːrl]

girl girl girl girl girl girl

---

child	[촤일드]	The child always wishes to be a man.	그 어린 아이는 항상 어른이 되기를 바래요.
citizen	[시티즌]	I am a Korean citizen.	나는 한국시민입니다.
course	[코-르스]	The full course is finished now.	전 과정이 이제 끝났어요.
friend	[프뤠ㄴ드]	I have many friends.	저는 친구가 많아요.
girl	[거얼]	That girl was wearing a blue skirt.	그 소녀는 파란 치마를 입고 있었다.

god
하느님
[gad]

god god god god

group
무리, 모임, 떼
[gruːp]

group group

idea
생각
[aidíːə]

idea idea idea idea

king
왕
[kiŋ]

king king king king

lady
숙녀, 부인
[léidi]

lady lady lady lady

god	[가드]	Oh, God.	오, 신이시여.
group	[구류웁]	Each group has its flag.	각 그룹마다 깃발이 있어요.
idea	[아이디어]	What a wonderful idea.	훌륭한 생각이다.
king	[킹]	The lion is the king of animals.	사자는 동물의 왕이에요.
lady	[레이디]	The lady over there is my aunt.	저기 있는 숙녀분은 우리 고모에요.

lead
인도하다
[iːd]

lead lead lead lead lead

letter
편지
[létər]

letter letter letter letter

life
생명, 생활
[lɑif]

life life life life life

live
살다
[liv]

live live live live live

luck
행운
[lɔk]

luck luck luck luck luck

lead	[리드]	Lead him to the place.	그를 그 장소로 인도하시오.
letter	[레러-ㄹ]	I send a letter to my friend Min-su.	나는 친구 민수에게 편지를 보내요.
life	[라이프]	Thank you for saving my life.	제 생명을 구해주셔서 감사해요.
live	[리브]	Where do you live?	사시는 곳이 어디예요?
luck	[럭]	Good luck!	행운을 빌어요!

mail
우편
[meil]

mail mail mail

man
남자
[mæn]

man man man man

marry
결혼하다
[mǽri]

marry marry marry marry

men
man의 복수형
[men]

men men men

Mrs.
~부인(여자 어른)
[mísiz]

Mrs. Mrs. Mrs. Mrs.

mail	[메일]	I send a letter by mail.	나는 편지를 우편으로 보낸다.
man	[맨]	The man is my father.	그 남자는 나의 아버지예요.
marry	[매뤼]	He will marry a woderful woman.	그는 멋진 여성과 결혼할 것이다.
men	[멘]	Most men like playing football.	대부분의 남자들은 축구하는 것을 좋아한다.
Mrs.	[미시즈]	Do you ever see Mrs. Kim?	김씨 부인을 본 적 있나요?

party
파티, 모임
[páːrti]

party　party　party　party

peace
평화
[piːs]

peace　peace　peace

people
사람들, 국민
[píːpl]

people　people　people

picnic
소풍
[píknik]

picnic　picnic　picnic

queen
여왕
[kwiːn]

queen queen queen

party	[파-ㄹ리]	Can you come to my party?	내 파티에 올래?
peace	[피-스]	I want the world peace.	나는 세계 평화를 원한다.
people	[피-쁠]	People like flowers.	사람들은 꽃을 좋아해요.
picnic	[피크닉]	We went on a picnic last weekend.	우리는 지난 주말에 소풍을 갔다.
queen	[퀴-ㄴ]	A queen is the wife of a king.	여왕은 왕의 아내이다.

sleep
잠자다
[sliːp]

sleep   sleep   sleep   sleep

stamp
우표, 인지
[stæmp]

stamp   stamp

story
이야기
[stɔ́ːri]

story   story   story   story

teenager
십대
[tíːneidʒər]

teenager   teenager

town
마을
[táun]

town   town   town   town

---

sleep	[슬리-입]	I went to sleep at 9 o'clock.	나는 9시에 잤어요.
stamp	[스탬프]	I like collecting stamps.	나는 우표 수집을 좋아해요.
story	[스토뤼]	The story is quite simple.	이야기는 간단하다.
teenager	[틴에이저-]	Teenagers really like music.	십대들은 음악을 정말 좋아한다.
town	[타운]	I live in town.	나는 마을에 살아요.

travel	travel travel travel
여행, 여행하다	
[trǽvəl]	

trip	trip trip trip trip
여행	
[trip]	

village	village village village
마을, 촌락	
[vílidʒ]	

welcome	welcome welcome
환영하다	
[wélkəm]	

woman	woman woman woman
여자	
[wúmən]	

travel	[튜뤠블]	I want to travel around the world.	나는 전세계를 여행하고 싶어요.
trip	[츄뤼ㅂ]	How was your trip?	이거 해보자!(이거 시도해보자)
village	[빌리쥐]	The farmer lives in the village.	그 농부는 마을에 살아요.
welcome	[웰컴]	Welcome to Korea!	한국에 오신 걸 환영합니다!
woman	[우먼]	A woman was singing in the street.	한 여자가 거리에서 노래 부르고 있어요.

3. 나, 너, 그...

I [아이]	I'm peter. I'm 10years old.	나는 Peter예요. 10살이죠.
my [마이]	This is my digital camera.	이것은 제 디지털카메라예요.
me [미-]	Look at me!	나를 보세요.
mine [마인]	The pen is mine.	그 펜은 내거야.

you	you you you you
너, 당신	
[juː]	

your	your your your your
너의, 너희들의	
[juər]	

yours	yours yours yours yours
너의 것	
[juərz]	

he	he he he he he
그는, 그가	
[hiː]	

hers	hers hers hers hers
그녀의 것	
[həːrz]	

you	[유-]	You look so pretty.	너는 굉장히 예쁘다(너는 참 예쁘구나).
your	[유얼]	What is your name?	너의 이름은 무엇이니?
yours	[유어즈]	Yours is beautiful.	너의 것은 예쁘다.
he	[히-]	He pointed the girl with a doll.	그는 인형을 가지고 있는 그 소녀를 가르켰어요.
hers	[허어즈]	This comic book is hers.	이 만화책은 그녀의 것이야.

21

herself
그녀 자신
[hərsélf]

herself　herself　herself

himself
그 자신, 그 스스로
[himself]

himself　himself　himself

his
그의, 그의 것
[híz]

his　his　his　his　his

him
그를, 그에게
[him]

him　him　him　him　him

she
그녀는, 그녀가
[ʃiː]

she　she　she　she

herself	[허셀프]	She did it herself.	그녀 자신이 그것을 했다
himself	[힘셀프]	He imagined himself a pilot.	자기가 조종사라고 상상했다.
his	[히이스]	It is his umbrella.	그것은 그의 우산이야.
him	[힘]	She loves him.	그녀는 그를 사랑해요.
she	[쉬]	She is really beautiful.	그녀는 정말 아름다워요.

| **her** 그녀의 [həːr] | her   her   her   her |  |

| **it** 그것은 [it] | it it it it it it it it |

| **its** 그것의 [its] | its its its its its its its its |

| **they** 그들은 [ðei] | they   they   they |  |

| **their** 그들의 [ðɛər] | their   their   their   their |

her	[허얼]	Jane is doing her homework.	Jane은 숙제하고 있어요.
it	[잇]	It is your dog.	그것은 당신의 강아지예요.
its	[잇즈]	The baby is sleeping in its bed.	갓난 아기는 침대에서 자고 있어요.
they	[데이]	They are going to school.	그들은 학교에 가고 있어요.
their	[데얼]	Their captain is very good.	그들의 주장은 굉장히 좋은 사람이야.

theirs 그들의 것 [ðɛər]	theirs theirs theirs
them 그들을 [ðem]	them them them 
we 우리, 저희가 [wiː]	we we we we we
yourself 너 자신,너 스스로 [juərsélf]	yourself yourself
our 우리의 [auər]	our our our our our our

theirs	[데얼]	Our customs are not like theirs.	우리의 습관은 그들과는 다르다
them	[뎀]	I told them to wait.	나는 그들에게 기다리라고 말했어요.
we	[위-]	We go to school at 8 o'clock.	우리는 8시에 등교한다.
yourself	[유어-셀프]	You must know yourself.	사람은 자기 자신을 알아야 한다.
our	[아우월]	That building is our school.	저 건물이 우리 학교야.

24

ours
우리의 것

[aʊərz]

ours　ours　ours　ours

ourselves

[àuərsélvz]

ourselves　　ourselves

us
우리들을

[ʌs]

us us us us us us us us

this
이것

[ðis]

this this this this this this

ours	[아워즈]	Which car is ours?	어느 것이 우리 차냐?
ourselves	[아우어 셀브즈]	We seated ourselves.	우리는 자리에 앉았다.
us	[어쓰]	He told us to stay home.	그는 우리에게 집에 있으라고 했다.
this	[디쓰]	How about this shirt?	이 셔츠는 어때요?

these 이것들 [ðíːz]

these these these

that 저것, 그것 [ðæt]

that that that that

those 그것들 [ðouz]

those those those those

themselves 그들 자신 [ðèmsélvz]

themselves themselves

these	[디-즈]	These apples are red.	이 사과들은 빨갛다.
that	[댓]	Look at that! That is big!	저것좀 봐! 크다!
those	[도즈]	Those shoes are expensive.	그 구두는 비싸다.
themselves	[그들 자신]	They made it themselves.	그들 자신이 그것을 만들었다.

4. 가족

baby
아기
[béibi]

baby   baby   baby   baby

brother
형제
[brʌ́ðr]

brother   brother   brother

cousin
사촌, 친척
[kʌ́zn]

cousin   cousin   cousin

dad/daddy
아빠
[dæd]

dad   dad   dad   dad   dad

baby	[베이비]	The baby girl is my little sister.	그 여자 아기는 내 여동생이예요.
brother	[브롸덜]	I have two younger brothers.	어린 남동생(형제)이 두 명 있어요.
cousin	[커즌]	This is my cousin, Mike.	얘는 내 사촌 Mike야.
dad/daddy	[대드]	Dad reads me some books at night.	아빠는 밤에 저에게 책을 읽어주셔요.

daughter
딸
[dɔ́ːtər]

daughter   daughter

family
가족
[fǽməli]

family   family

father
아버지
[fáːðər]

father father father father

grandmother
할머니
[grǽndmáːðər]

grandmother

husband
남편
[hʌ́zbənd]

husband   husband

---

daughter [더-러] My aunt has two daughters and a son.   우리 이모는 1남 2녀(아들한명과 두 딸)를 두셨어요.

family [페믈리] This is a picture of my family.   우리 가족 사진이예요.

father [퐈-덜] I love my father.   전 아빠를 사랑해요.

grandmother [그랜드머더] Grandmother likes to tell me interesting story.   할머니는 저에게 재밌는 얘기 해주시는 걸 좋아하셔요.

husband [허즈번드] I love my husband.   나는 내 남편을 사랑해요.

ma'am
아주머니, 선생님(여교사)

[məm]

ma'am   ma'am   ma'am

mom
엄마

[mam]

mom   mom   mom   mom

mother
어머니

[mʌ́ðər]

mother   mother

nephew
조카

[néfjː]

nephew   nephew

parent
부모님

[pɛ́ərənt]

parent   parent   parent

---

ma'am	[맴]	-Min-ho. -Yes, ma'am.	민호야. 예, 선생님.
mom	[맘]	Mom got angry with me.	어머니가 나에게 화가 나셨다.
mother	[머덜]	She is my mother.	그녀는 나의 어머니예요.
nephew	[비퓨-]	I like my nephews.	나는 조카들을 좋아한다.
parent	[페어뤄ㄴ트]	My parents are very nice.	나의 부모님은 매우 좋으신 분이예요.

relatives
친척
[rélətivz]

relatives   relatives

sister
여자형제, 언니
[sístər]

sister sister sister

son
아들
[sɔn]

son   son   son   son   son

uncle
아저씨, 삼촌
[ʌ́ŋkl]

uncle   uncle   uncle

wife
부인
[wáif]

wife   wife   wife   wife

relatives [렐러티브즈]	Do you have many relatives?	당신은 친척들이 많이 있나요?
sister [씨스털]	I have two sisters.	나는 두 명의 여자형제가 있어요.
son [썬]	He is my son.	그는 나의 아들이다.
uncle [엉끌]	I am going to my uncle's.	나는 삼촌댁에 갈 거예요.
wife [와이프]	She is my wife.	그녀는 제 아내입니다.

5. 우리 몸

arm
팔
[aːrm]

arm　arm　arm　arm

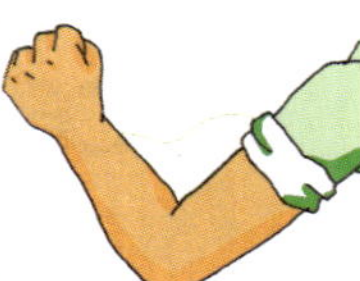

back
등, 뒤
[bæk]

back　back　back　back

body
몸, 신체
[bádi]

body　body　body

ear
귀
[iər]

ear　ear　ear　ear　ear　ear

arm	[아-ㄹ암]	Tom's arm is long.	Tom은 팔이 길어요.
back	[백]	I looked at his back.	난 그의 등을 보았어요.
body	[바디]	My whole body is aching now.	지금 온몸이 아파요.
ear	[이얼]	Rabbits have long ears.	토끼의 귀는 길어요.

eye
눈
[ai]

eye eye eye eye eye

face
얼굴
[feis]

face face face face

finger
손가락
[fíŋɡər]

finger finger finger

foot
발
[fut]

foot foot foot

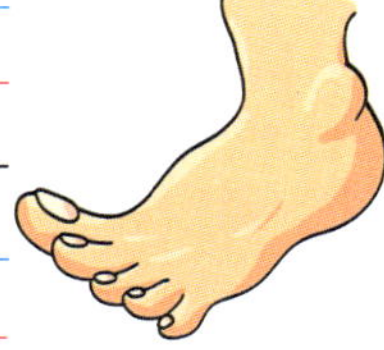

hair
머리카락, 털
[hɛər]

hair hair hair hair hair

eye	[아이]	Open your eyes and look around.	눈을 뜨고 주위를 둘러보세요.
face	[푸페이스]	I wash my face everyday.	나는 매일 얼굴을 씻어요(세수해요).
finger	[휭거ㄹ]	I touched water with my fingers.	손가락으로 물을 만져보았어요.
foot	[풋]	Peter is pushing the box with his foot.	Peter는 발로 상자를 밀고 있다.
hair	[헤얼]	Her hair is black and short.	그녀의 머리카락은 검고 짧아.

hand	hand hand hand hand
손	
[hænd]	

head	head head head
머리	
[hed]	

heart	heart heart heart heart
마음, 심장	
[hɑːrt]	

knee	knee knee knee
무릎	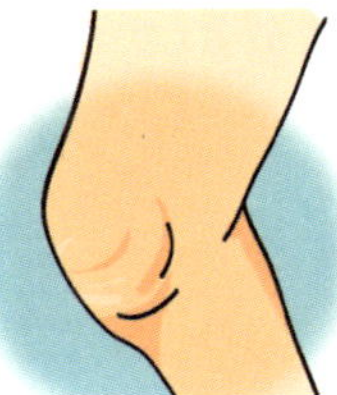
[niː]	

leg	leg leg leg leg leg
다리	
[leg]	

---

hand	[핸드]	We must wash our hands.	손을 꼭 씻어야 해요.
head	[헤드]	His head touches the ceiling.	그의 머리는 천장에 닿아요.
heart	[하-르트]	The doctor is checking my heart.	의사 선생님이 제 심장을 검사하고 계세요.
knee	[니-]	I feel pain in my knee.	무릎이 아파요.
leg	[렉]	I broke my leg three days ago.	3일전에 다리가 부러졌어요.

lip
입술
[lip]

lip lip lip lip lip lip

mouth
입
[mauθ]

mouth   mouth

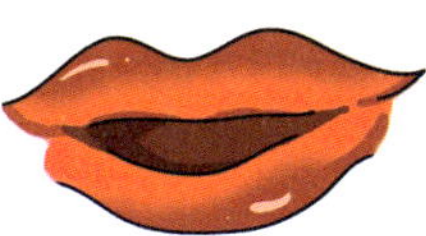

neck
목
[nek]

neck neck neck neck

nose
코
[nouz]

nose nose nose

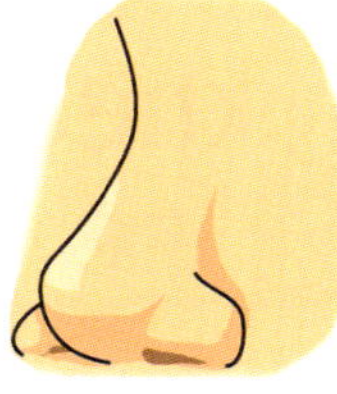

tooth
이, 치아
[tuːθ]

tooth tooth tooth tooth

lip	[립]	Her lips turned purple with cold.	추워서 그의 입술이 자줏빛이 되었다.
mouth	[마웃쓰]	Tom opened his mouth.	Tom은 입을 벌렸어요.
neck	[넥]	A neck is a part of our body.	목은 우리 몸의 한 부분이다.
nose	[노우즈]	We have a nose.	우리는 하나의 코를 가지고 있다.
tooth	[투-쓰]	Brush your tooth before you go to bed.	자기전 이를 닦아라.

6. 집과 가구

bed
침대
[bed]

bed　bed　bed

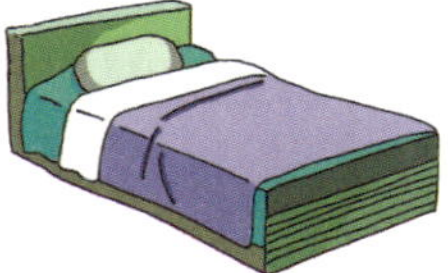

bell
종, 초인종
[bel]

bell bell bell bell bell bell

bench
긴 의자, 벤치
[bentʃ]

bench　bench　bench

chair
의자
[tʃɛər]

chair　chair　chair

bed	[뱃]	We have three beds.	우리는 침대가 3개 있어요.
bell	[벨]	Listen! The bell is ringing.	들어봐~ 종이 울리고 있어.
bench	[벤취]	There are three benches in the park.	공원에는 벤치가 3개 있다.
chair	[췌어ㄹ]	There is a cat under the chair.	의자 밑에 고양이 한 마리가 있어요.

curtain 커튼 [kə́ːrtn]	curtain curtain curtain
door 문 [dɔːr]	door door door door
garden 정원 [gáːrdn]	garden garden garden
gas 가스 [gæs]	gas gas gas gas
glass 유리, 유리컵 [glæs]	glass glass glass glass

curtain	[커튼]	I hid behind the curtain.	전 커튼 뒤로 숨었어요.
door	[도얼]	I knocked on the door.	나는 문을 두드렸어요.
garden	[가-ㄹ든]	There are roses in that garden.	저 정원엔 장미가 있어요.
gas	[개스]	We filled the ballon with gas.	우리는 풍선에 가스를 채웠다.
glass	[글래쓰]	I drink three glasses of milk everyday.	나는 매일 우유를 세 잔씩 마셔요.

hall 현관 [hɔ́ː]	hall hall hall hall	
home 집 [hóum]	home home home	
house 집 [haus]	house house house	
key 열쇠 [kiː]	key key key key key	
kitchen 부엌 [kítʃin]	kitchen kitchen kitchen	

hall	[홀]	A city hall.	시청
home	[홈]	I have to stay at home today.	나는 오늘 집에 있어야만 해요.
house	[하우스]	There is a big house on the hill.	언덕위에는 큰 집이 한 채 있어요.
key	[키-]	I lost my key yesterday.	저는 어제 열쇠를 잃어버렸어요.
kitchen	[킷췬]	Refrigerator is in the kitchen.	냉장고는 부엌에 있어요.

knife
칼
[naif]

knife   knife   knife   knife

room
방
[ruːm]

room   room   room

soap
비누
[soup]

soap   soap   soap   soap

sofa
소파
[sóufə]

sofa   sofa   sofa

stair
계단
[stέər]

stair   stair   stair   stair

knife	[나이프]	The knife is dangerous.	그 칼은 위험해요.
room	[루-움]	I usually study in my room.	나는 보통 내 방에서 공부해요.
soap	[쏘웁]	Wash your hand with soap.	비누로 손을 깨끗이 씻어라.
sofa	[쏘우풔]	The cushion is on the sofa.	그 쿠션은 소파 위에 있다.
stair	[스떼어]	I went up stairs.	나는 계단을 올랐다.

7. 직업

captain
선장, 우두머리
[kǽptin]

captain captain captain

cook
요리사
[kúk]

cook cook cook

doctor
의사
[dάktər]

doctor doctor doctor

farmer
농부
[fάːrmər]

farmer farmer farmer

captain	[캡틴]	Mr. Han is the captain of the soccer team.	한선생님은 그 축구팀의 주장이에요.
cook	[쿡]	My mom is a great cook.	우리 엄마는 훌륭한 요리사다.
doctor	[닥터ㄹ]	I would like to be a doctor.	나는 의사가 되고 싶어요.
farmer	[파-머-]	The farmer loves art.	농부는 예술을 사랑한답니다.

fisherman 어부 [fíʃərmən]	fisherman　fisherman
job 일, 직업 [dʒab]	job job job job job job
model 모델 [mɔ́dl]	model model model model
nurse 간호사 [nəːrs]	nurse nurse nurse 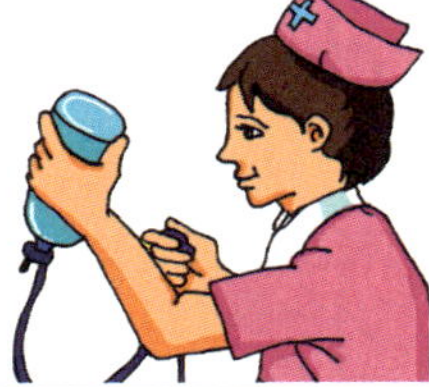
pilot 조종사 [páilət]	pilot pilot pilot pilot pilot

fisherman [피셔-먼]	The fisherman launched.	그 어부는 고기를 잡으러 갔다.
job [쟙]	"What's her job?"	그녀의 직업은 무엇인가요?
model [모들]	I will be your model.	내가 모델이 되어주마
nurse [널쓰]	She is a nurse.	그녀는 간호사이다.
pilot [파일럿]	I want to be a pilot.	나는 조종사가 되고 싶어요.

| **police** 경찰 [pəlíːs] | police police police |  |

police police police

| **reporter** 기자 [ripɔ́ːrtər] |

reporter reporter reporter

| **scientist** 과학자 [sáiəntist] |

scientist   scientist

| **stewardess** 스튜어디스 [stjúːərdis] |

stewardess   stewardess

| **talent** 탤런트 [tǽlənt] |

talent talent talent talent

---

police	[펄리-스]	Police caught a thief.	경찰이 도둑을 잡았어요.
reporter	[리포-터-]	This is a reporter of the CNN.	저는 CNN의 기자입니다.
scientist	[사이언티스트]	He is an eminent scientist.	그는 훌륭한 과학자입니다.
srewardess	[스튜어-디스]	I want to be a stewardess.	저는 스튜어디스가 되고 싶습니다.
talent	[탤런트]	He is well-known talent.	그는 유명한 탤런트입니다.

41

8. 식사와 음식

butter
버터
[bʌ́tər]

butter butter butter butter

breakfast
아침식사
[brékfəst]

breakfast   breakfast

bread
빵
[bred]

bread bread bread

cake
케이크
[keik]

cake   cake   cake   cake

butter	[버러r]	There are bread and butter.	빵과 버터가 있어요.
breakfast	[브뢰ㄱ풔스트]	I ate bread and milk for breakfast.	나는 아침으로 빵과 우유를 먹었다.
bread	[브레드]	Tom, would like some bread?	Tom, 빵 좀 먹을래?
cake	[케이크]	She gave me a piece of cake.	그녀는 나에게 케이크 한 조각을 주었다.

candy 사탕 [kǽndi]	candy candy candy candy
cheese 치즈 [tʃiːz]	cheese cheese cheese
coffee 커피 [kɔ́ːfi]	coffee coffee coffee 
cream 크림 [kriːm]	cream cream cream
dinner 저녁 식사 [dínər]	dinner dinner dinner

candy	[캔디]	Andy gave me a candy.	Andy가 나에게 사탕을 주었어요.
cheese	[취즈]	Mice are eating cheese.	쥐들이 치즈를 먹고 있어요.
coffee	[커-퓌]	Give me a cup of coffee.	커피 한 잔 주세요.
cream	[크뤼-임]	Put two spoons of cream.	크림 두 스푼을 넣으세요.
dinner	[디널]	I had dinner with my friend, Tony.	나는 친구 Tony와 저녁을 먹었어요.

egg
달걀
[eg]

egg egg egg egg egg egg

food
음식
[fuːd]

food food food food

ham
햄
[hǽm]

ham ham ham ham

hamburger
햄버거
[hǽmbəːrgər]

hamburger hamburger

hot dog
핫도그
[hát dɔ́ːg]

hot dog hot dog hot dog

egg	[엑]	Chickens lay an egg each morning.	닭은 매일 아침 달걀을 한 개씩 낳아요.
food	[푸-드]	What is your favorite food?	좋아하는 음식은 무엇인가요?
ham	[햄]	I made your favorite, ham.	당신이 제일 좋아하는 햄을 만들었어.
hamburger	[햄버거]	Are you eating hamburger again?	너 햄버거 또 먹는거야?
hot dog	[핫 독]	We had hot dogs for lunch today.	우리는 오늘 점심으로 핫도그를 먹었다.

jam
잼
[dʒæm]

jam   jam   jam   jam

Juice
주스
[dʒúːs]

juice   juice   juice

meat
고기
[miːt]

meat   meat   meat   meat

milk
우유
[milk]

milk   milk   milk   milk

pizza
피자
[píːtsə]

pizza   pizza   pizza   pizza

jam	[잼]	He spread jam on bread.	그는 빵에 잼을 발랐다.
juice	[쥬-스]	Would you like some juice?	주스 좀 드실래요?
meat	[미-잇트]	We will have meat for dinner.	우리는 저녁식사로 고기를 먹을 거야.
milk	[밀크]	Milk is good for our health.	우유는 건강에 좋다.
pizza	[핏쩌]	We had the pizza delivered.	우리는 피자를 배달시켰다.

pork 돼지고기 [pɔ́ːrk]	pork pork pork pork
rice 쌀, 밥 [rais]	rice rice rice rice rice
salad 샐러드 [sǽləd]	salad salad salad 
salt 소금 [sɔːlt]	salt salt salt salt salt
sandwich 샌드위치 [sǽndwitʃ]	sandwich sandwich

pork	[포-크]	Muslims do not eat pork.	이슬람교도는 돼지고기를 먹지 않는다.
rice	[라이스]	Korean usually eat rice.	한국 사람들은 보통 밥을 먹는다.
salad	[쌜러드]	I ate some salad and chicken.	나는 샐러드와 치킨을 먹었다.
salt	[써-얼트]	Could you pass me the salt, please.	소금 좀 건내 주시겠어요?
sandwich	[쌘드위치]	I'd like a ham sandwich and coffee.	햄 샌드위치와 커피 주세요.

46

sausage 소시지 [sɔ́:sidʒ]	sausage sausage sausage
soup 소프 [súːp]	soup soup soup soup
spaghetti 스파게티 [spəgéti]	spaghetti spaghetti
sugar 설탕 [ʃúgər]	sugar sugar sugar sugar
supper 저녁식사 [sʌ́pər]	supper supper supper

sausage	[써-씨쥐]	We eat pork sausage for breakfast.	우리는 아침 식사로 돼지고기 소시지를 먹는다.
soup	[쑤웁]	Would you like some soup?	수프 좀 드시겠어요?
spaghetti	[스파게티]	Shall we order spaghetti?	스타게티 시킬까요?
sugar	[슈걸]	Do you like sugar in your coffee?	커피에 설탕 넣으시겠어요?
supper	[써퍼얼]	Supper is the last meal of the day.	저녁식사는 하루의 마지막 식사이다.

9. 과일과 야채

apple
사과
[æpəl]

apple apple apple

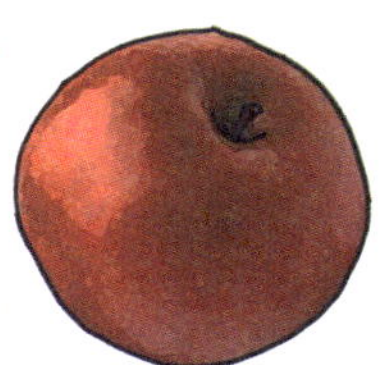

banana
바나나
[bənǽnə]

banana banana

cabbage
양배추
[kǽbidʒ]

cabbage cabbage cabbage

carrot
당근
[kǽrət]

carrot carrot carrot carrot

apple	[애쁠]	Do you like apples?	사과 좋아하세요?
banana	[버내너]	I like bananas very much.	나는 바나나를 무척 좋아해요.
cabbage	[캐비지]	The man is chopping up the cabbage.	남자는 양배추를 썰고 있다.
carrot	[캐럿]	My hamster likes to eat carrots.	내 햄스터는 당근을 즐겨 먹는다.

corn
옥수수
[kɔːrn]

corn corn corn corn corn

cucumber
오이
[kjúːkʌmbər]

cucumber   cucumber

fruit
과일
[fruːt]

fruit fruit fruit fruit fruit

grape
포도
[greip]

grape   grape   grape

melon
메론
[mélən]

melon melon melon melon

corn	[콘]	Do you like corn?	옥수수 좋아하세요?
cucumber	[큐컴벌]	A cucumber is long and green.	오이는 길고 녹색이다.
fruit	[푸룻-ㅌ]	What is your favorite fruit?	좋아하는 과일이 무엇인가요?
grape	[그뢰입]	Does Peter like grapes?	Peter는 포도를 좋아하나요?
melon	[메런]	Melons are in full flush.	멜론이 한물졌다.

onion
양파
[ʌ́njən]

onion onion onion onion

peach
복숭아
[píːtʃ]

peach peach peach peach

pear
(과일)배
[pɛə́r]

pear pear pear pear

pineapple
파인애플
[páinæpl]

pineapple pineapple

potato
감자
[pətéitou]

potato potato potato

---

onion	[어니언]	Hold the onions with my burger.	제 버거에는 양파를 생략해 주세요.
peach	[피-치]	I'm allergic to peaches.	나는 복숭아 알레르기가 있어요.
pear	[페얼]	This pear is sweet.	이 배는 달다.
pineapple	[파인애쁠]	Do you like eating pineapples?	여러분은 파인애플 먹는 것을 좋아하나요?
potato	[퍼테이토우]	I'll have the baked potato.	구운 감자를 먹겠습니다.

spinach 시금치 [spínitʃ]	spinach spinach spinach
strawberry 딸기 [strɔ́ːbéri]	strawberry strawberry
tomato 토마토 [təméitou]	tomato tomato tomato
sweet potato 고구마 [swíːt pətéitou]	sweet potato sweet potato
vegetable 야채 [védʒətəbl]	vegetable vegetable

spinach [스피니치]	Spinach is rich in iron.	시금치에는 철분이 풍부하다.
strawberry [쓰루-베뤼]	I like strawberry.	나는 딸기를 좋아해요.
tomato [터메이토]	My mother likes tomato juice.	엄마는 토마토주스를 좋아하세요.
sweet potato [스윗퍼테이토우]	I steamed the sweet potatoes.	고구마를 쪘어요.
vegetable [붸쥐터블]	All the vegetables are fresh.	야채가 참 신선합니다.

10. 옷과 악세서리

button
단추, 버튼
[bʌ́tn]

button　button　button

cap
모자
[kæp]

cap　cap　cap　cap

clothes
옷
[klouðz]

clothes　clothes　clothes

coat
외투
[kout]

coat　coat　coat　coat　coat

button	[버튼]	The baby is touching the buttons.	아기가 단추를 만지고 있어요.
cap	[캡]	Mom bought me this cap.	엄마가 이 모자를 사주셨어요.
clothes	[클로우즈]	I'm making clothes for my cat.	지금 제 고양이에게 입힐 옷을 만들고 있어요.
coat	[코웃]	My grandfather bought me a blue coat.	할아버지께서 파란색 코트를 사주셨어요.

dress
의복

[dres]

dress dress dress

glove
장갑

[glʌv]

glove glove glove glove

hat
모자

[hæt]

hat hat hat hat

jacket
재킷

[dʒækit]

jacket jacket jacket

pants
바지

[pænts]

pants pants pants

dress	[드뤼스]	I want to wear the pink dress.	분홍색 드레스(옷)를 입고 싶어요.
glove	[글러브]	I left my gloves at home.	내 장갑을 집에 두고 왔어요.
hat	[햇]	Mrs. Lee always wears a hat.	이 선생님은 항상 모자를 쓰고 다니셔요.
jacke	[줴킷]	I really like that jacket.	그 재킷 정말 맘에 든다.
pants	[팬츠]	Tom always wear same pants.	탐은 항상 같은 바지를 입어.

ribbon 리본 [ríbə]	ribbon　　ribbon	

ring 반지 [riŋ]	ring　　ring　　ring	

sandals 샌들 [sǽndlz]	sandals　sandals　sandals

shirt 셔츠 [ʃə:rt]	shirt　shirt　shirt　shirt

shoe 신, 구두 [ʃuː]	shoe　shoe　shoe　shoe

ribbon	[뤼번]	She wears red ribbon on her hair.	그녀는 머리에 빨간 리본을 하고 있다.
ring	[륑]	He gave me a ring.	그가 나에게 반지를 주었어요.
sandals	[샌들즈]	On his feet, he wore sandals.	그는 발에 샌들을 신었다.
shirt	[셔-ㄹ츠]	I bought this shirt last year.	작년에 이 셔츠를 샀어요.
shoe	[슈-]	My father bought a pair of shoes for me.	아빠가 저에게 신발(한켤레)을 사주셨어요.

skirt
스커트
[skə:rt]

skirt　skirt　skirt

sock
양말
[sak]

sock sock sock sock sock

suit
정장
[súːt]

suit　suit　suit　suit

sweater
스웨터
[swétər]

sweater　sweater　sweater

swimsuit
수영복
[swímsùːt]

swimsuit　　swimsuit

skirt	[스꺼얼트]	That skirt looks cool.	저 치마 멋져보여.
sock	[싹]	I'm looking for my red socks.	나는 내 빨간 양말을 찾고 있다.
suit	[수-트]	He likes to wear suits.	그는 정장 입는 것을 좋아합니다.
sweater	[스웨터]	This sweater is warm.	이 스웨터는 따뜻하다.
swimsuit	[스임수-트]	Where is my swimsuit?	내 수영복은 어디 있어요?

11. 도시와 건축물

airport
공항
[ɛ́ərpɔ̀ːrt]

airport   airport

bakery
빵집
[béikəri]

bakery   bakery   bakery

bank
은행
[bæŋk]

bank   bank   bank

bookstore
서점
[búkstɔ́ːr]

bookstore   bookstore

airport	[에어포-르트]	Is there a bus to airport?	공항으로 가는 버스가 있어요?
bakery	[베이커리]	I would love to run a bakery.	나는 빵집을 운영하고 싶다.
bank	[뱅크]	My father works for that bank.	우리 아빠는 저 은행에서 일하세요.
bookstore	[북스토어-]	Is there a bookstore around here?	근처에 서점이 있습니까?

bridge 다리 [bridʒ]	bridge bridge	
capital 수도, 서울 [kǽpitl]	capital capital capital	
church 교회 [tʃəːtʃ]	church church	
city 도시 [síti]	city city city city city city	
coffee shop 커피 판매점 [kɔ́ːfi ʃáp]	coffee shop coffee shop	

bridge [브릿쥐]　We walked across the bridge.　우리는 걸어서 다리를 건넜어요.
capital [캐피틀]　Seoul is the capital of Korea.　서울은 대한민국의 수도예요.
church [춰-ㄹ춰]　I go to church on Sundays.　저는 일요일마다 교회에 가요.
city [씨티]　There are lots of people in the city.　이 도시에는 사람들이 아주 많아요.
coffee shop [코-피샵]　I'll be waiting at the coffee shop.　커피숍에서 기다리고 있을게.

fire station
소방서

[fáiərstéiʃən]

fire station   fire station

hospital
병원

[háspitl]

hospital hospital hospital

hotel
호텔

[houtél]

hotel hotel hotel hotel

library
도서관

[láibrəri]

library library library

office
사무실

[ɔ́ːfis]

office office office

fire station [브릿쥐]	My house is near the fire station.	우리집은 소방서 근처에 있습니다.
hospital [하스피틀]	Ted is in the hospital.	Ted는 병원에 입원해 있어요.
hotel [호텔]	How about staying in a hotel?	호텔에 묵는 건 어때요?
library [라이브러리]	They study at home or in the library.	그들은 집이나 도서관에서 공부해요.
office [어-퓌스]	He works hard in his office.	그는 그의 사무실에서 열심히 일한다.

park
공원
[páːrk]

park park park park

place
장소, 곳
[pleis]

place place place place

post office
우체국
[póust óːfis]

post office post office

restaurant
레스토랑
[réstərənt]

restaurant restaurant

road
길, 도로
[roud]

road road road

park	[파-크]	The city also has many parks.	이 도시에는 공원도 많이 있습니다.
place	[플레이스]	The place is very nice.	그 장소는 매우 멋져.
post office	[포스트 어-퓌스]	The post office is near the station.	우체국은 역 부근에 있다.
restaurant	[뤠스토뢴트드]	We had a dinner at restaurant.	우리는 레스토랑에서 저녁을 먹었어요.
road	[로우드]	The road is narrow.	그 도로는 좁아요.

seat	seat seat seat seat
자리, 좌석	
[siːt]	

station	station station
역, 정거장	
[stéiʃən]	

street	street street street street
거리	
[strit]	

theater	theater theater theater
극장	
[θíːətər]	

---

seat	[씨-잇트]	Please, have a seat.	앉으세요.
station	[스때이션]	I wait for taxi at the station.	나는 정거장에서 택시를 기다린다.
street	[스뜨뤼-ㅅ]	Let's cross the street.	길을 건너자.
theater	[씨-어터-]	He went into the movie theater.	그녀는 영화관에 들어갔다.

black 검은 색 [blæk]

black black black black

beige 베이지 색 [béʒ]

beige beige beige beige

blue 파란색 [bluː]

blue blue blue

brown 갈색, 갈색의 [braun]

brown brown brown

black	[블랙]	The prince has black hair.	왕자 머리카락은 검은색이에요.
beige	[베이지]	He was wearing a beige suit.	그는 베이지색 양복을 입고 있었다.
blue	[블루-]	Jessica has blue eyes.	Jessica의 눈은 파란색이예요.
brown	[브롸운]	My teacher wears brown jacket.	선생님은 갈색 자켓을 입고 계시다.

color	color color color color
색깔	
[kʌ́lər]	

gray	gray gray gray gray
회색, 회색의	
[grei]	

green	green green green green
녹색	
[griːn]	

orange	orange orange
오렌지 색	
[ɔ́ːrindʒ]	

pink	pink pink pink pink
분홍	
[piŋk]	

color	[컬러르]	What is your favorite color?	가장 좋아하는 색이 뭐야?
gray	[그뢰이]	I like this gray sweater.	나는 이 회색 스웨터가 좋아.
green	[그뤼인]	I like green color.	저는 녹색을 좋아해요.
orange	[오륀쥐]	Where is my orange shirt?	내 오렌지색 셔츠 어디 있니?
pink	[핑크]	I like the pink.	나는 분홍색을 좋아해요.

purple

보라색

[pə́:rpl]

purple purple purple

red

빨간색, 붉은

[red]

red red red red red red

silver

은빛

[silvər]

silver silver silver silver

white

흰, 흰빛

[hwait]

white white white white

yellow

노랑

[jélou]

yellow yellow

purple	[퍼-플]	Purple isn't her color.	보라색은 그녀에게 안 어울려.
red	[뤠드]	She was red with shame.	그녀는 부끄러워서 얼굴이 빨개졌다.
silver	[실버]	He gave me a silver ring.	그는 나에게 은반지를 주었다.
white	[와이트]	We can see the white color in the dark.	우리는 어둠 속에서 흰색을 볼 수 있다.
yellow	[옐로-]	The banana is yellow.	바나나는 노랑색이다.

63

13. 때와 계절

| afternoon 오후 [æftərnúːn] | afternoon afternoon |  |

| A.M. 오전 [éiém] | A.M. A.M. A.M. A.M. |

| April 4월 [éiprəl] | April April April April |

| autumn 가을 [ɔ́ːtəm] | autumn autumn |  |

---

afternoon [애프터누-운] I met him in the afternoon. 나는 그를 오후에 만났어요.

A.M. [에이엠] It's almost 10 A.M. 오전 10시가 다 되었어요.

April [에이쁘럴] I was born in April. 나는 4월에 태어났어요.

autumn [어-틈] It is windy in the autumn. 가을에는 바람이 많이 불어요.

calendar 달력 [kǽləndər]	calendar calendar
date 날짜 [deit]	date date date 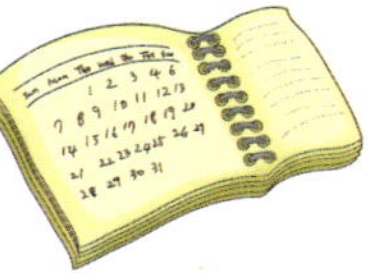
day 낮, 하루 [dei]	day day day day day day
evening 저녁 [íːvniŋ]	evening evening 
everyday 매일 [évridèi]	everyday everyday

calendar [캘린더얼]	There is a calendar on the wall.	벽에 달력이 있어요.
date [데잇트]	What's the date today?	오늘 몇일이에요?(오늘 날짜가 어떻게 되죠?)
day [데이]	I play all day long every day.	난 매일 하루 종일 놀아요.
evening [이-브닝]	I feel tired in the evening.	나는 저녁에는 피곤해.
everyday [에브리데이]	You should study hard everyday.	너는 매일 열심히 공부해야 한다.

fall
가을
[fɔːl]

fall fall fall fall fall fall

holiday
휴일, 공휴일
[hálədéi]

holiday holiday holiday

lunch
점심
[lʌntʃ]

lunch lunch lunch lunch

month
달
[mʌnθ]

month month month

morning
아침
[mɔ́ːrniŋ]

morning morning

fall	[풔ㄹ]	In fall, we can see many leaves.	가을에는 낙엽을 많이 볼 수 있어요.
holiday	[할러데이]	Did you have a good holiday?	휴일 잘 보내셨어요?
lunch	[런취]	It's time for lunch.	점심 먹을 시간이에요.
month	[먼쓰]	I go to movies once a month.	나는 한 달에 한 번 영화를 보러 가요.
morning	[모-ㄹ닝]	Good morning!	좋은 아침!

night 밤 [nait]	night night night	
noon 정오, 한 낮 [nuːn]	noon noon noon noon	
season 계절 [síːzn]	season season season	
P.M. 오후 [píːém]	P.M. P.M. P.M. P.M.	
spring 봄 [spriŋ]	spring spring	

night	[나잇]	I stayed up all night.	나는 밤새도록 깨어 있었다.
noon	[눈]	We have lunch at noon.	우리는 정오에 점심을 먹는다.
season	[씨-즌]	What's your favorite season?	가장 좋아하는 계절은?
P.M.	[피-엠]	Let's meet at 8 P.M.	오후 8시에 만나죠.
spring	[스프링]	I like spring.	난 봄이 좋아요.

| **summer** 여름 [sʌ́mər] | summer   summer |  |

| **today** 오늘 [tudéi] | today   today   today |

| **tomorrow** 내일 [təmɔ́ːrou] | tomorrow   tomorrow |

| **tonight** 오늘 밤 [tənáit] | tonight   tonight   tonight |

| **week** 주, 1주간 [wiːk] | week   week   week   week |

---

summer	[써머ㄹ]	In summer, it is hot.	여름에는 더워요.
today	[투데이]	Today is my birthday.	오늘은 내 생일이다.
tomorrow	[투머-로우]	Tomorrow will be cold.	내일은 추울 거야.
tonight	[터나잇]	Tonight will be snowy.	오늘밤엔 눈이 올 거야.
week	[위-크]	I will travel America for a week.	나는 일주일동안 미국을 여행할 거야.

weekend 주말 [wíːkènd]	weekend weekend
winter 겨울 [wíntər]	winter winter winter 
year 년, 나이 [jiər]	year year year year
yesterday 어제 [jéstərdéi]	yesterday yesterday 
zero 0, 영 [zíərou]	zero zero zero zero

weekend	[위-켄드]	Want to see a movie this weekend?	이번 주말에 영화 볼래요?
winter	[원터얼]	It's cold in winter.	겨울엔 추워요.
year	[이얼]	Happy new year!	새해 복 많이 받으세요!
yesterday	[예스털데이]	Yesterday was my brother's birthday.	어제는 내 남동생의 생일이었다.
zero	[지로우]	'0' is called zero.	0은 영이라고 부른다.

14. 시간과 방향

age
나이
[eidʒ]

age　age　age　age　age

east
동쪽
[iːst]

east　east　east

four
4, 4의
[fɔːr]

four　four　four　four　four

half
반, 2분의1
[hæf]

half　half　half　half　half

age	[에이쥐]	At the age of 10, I went to Italy.	열살 때 저는 이탈리아로 갔어요.
east	[이스트]	Go east.	동쪽으로 가.
four	[포-]	My family is four.	우리 가족은 4명입니다.
half	[해프]	Please cut this bread in half.	이 빵을 반으로 잘라주세요.

| **hour**
시간
[auər] | hour　hour　hour |  |

| **hundred**
백(100)
[hʌ́ndrəd] | hundred　　hundred |

| **map**
지도
[mæp] | map　map　map　map |

| **minute**
분
[mínit] | minute　minute　minute |

| **million**
100만
[míljən] | million　million　million |

hour	[아우월]	Peter slept for five **hours**.	Peter는 5시간동안 잤어요.
hundred	[헌드뤗]	My grandfather is one **hundred** years old.	할아버지는 100세이십니다.
map	[맵]	I marked my house on the **map**.	우리(나의)집을 지도에 표시했다.
minute	[미닛]	We have only 5 **minutes**.	우리는 오직 5분의 시간이 없어(우리는 5분밖에 시간이 없어).
million	[밀리언]	He has one **million** won.	그는 백만 원이 있어요.

north
북쪽
[nɔːrθ]

north　north　north　north

number
수, 숫자
[nʌmbər]

number　number

o'clock
~시(정각)
[əklák]

o'clock　　o'clock

set
한 벌, 짝, 세트
[set]

set　set　set　set　set

south
남쪽
[sauθ]

south　south　south

north	[노-르쓰]	My house stands in the north of Seoul.	우리 집은 서울의 북쪽에 있다.
numbe r	[넘벌]	The number is two.	그 숫자는 2이다.
o'clock	[어클락]	It is 6 o'clock.	6시예요.
set	[세엣]	I have a set of gloves.	나는 장갑 한 쌍이 있다.
south	[싸웃쓰]	The man went south.	그는 남쪽으로 갔다.

time
시각, 시간
[taim]

time time time time

visit
방문하다
[vízit]

visit visit visit visit

way
길, 방법
[wei]

way way way way

west
서쪽
[west]

west west west west

time	[타임]	What time is it?	지금 몇 시죠?
visit	[뷔짓]	Can you visit me, today?	오늘 절 방문해 줄 수 있나요?
way	[웨이]	There is no way through.	통로가 없어요.
west	[웨스트]	The sun sets in the west.	해는 서쪽으로 진다.

15. 식물

carnation
카네이션
[kɑːrnéiʃən]

carnation   carnation

flower
꽃
[fláuər]

flower   flower   flower

grain
곡식
[gréin]

grain   grain   grain   grain

grass
풀
[grǽs]

grass   grass   grass

---

carnation [카-네이션] I also gave them red carnations. 빨강 카네이션도 드렸지.

flower [플라워-] Tulips are a spring flower. 튤립은 봄에 꽃이 핀다.

grain [그레인] They learned how to grow grains. 그들은 곡식을 재배하는 법을 배웠다.

grass [그뢰스] I lay down on the grass. 나는 풀 밭에 누웠습니다.

leaf
잎
[líːf]

leaf leaf leaf leaf

lily
백합
[líli]

lily lily lily lily lily lily

pine
소나무
[páin]

pine pine pine pine

plant
식물
[plǽnt]

plant plant plant plant

rose
장미
[róuz]

rose rose rose rose

leaf	[리-프]	I picked up a fallen leaf.	나는 낙엽을 주웠다.
lily	[릴리]	He plucked a lily for her.	그는 그녀에게 백합꽃을 꺾어 주었다
pine	[파인]	There is the pine forest.	이곳에는 소나무숲이 있다.
plant	[플랜트]	Plants like water.	식물은 물을 좋아한다.
rose	[로우즈]	Roses are beautiful.	장미는 아름답다.

sunflower 해바라기 [sʌ́nflàuər]	sunflower　sunflower
tulip 튤립 [tjúːlip]	tulip　tulip　tulip　tulip
vine 덩굴 [vain]	vine　vine　vine　vine
weed 잡초 [wíːd]	weed　weed　weed　weed
wheat 밀 [hwíːt]	wheat　wheat　wheat

sunflower	[선플라워-]	The sunflower turns towards sun.	해바라기는 태양을 향한다.
tulip	[튤립]	The flowers I like are lilies and tulips.	내가 좋아하는 꽃은 백합과 튤립이에요.
vine	[바인]	A vine bleeds when it is cut.	덩굴은 자르면 수액이 나온다.
weed	[위-드]	The garden wants to be weeded.	정원은 제초가 되어야 한다.
wheat	[위-트]	It is hard to tell wheat from barley.	밀과 보리를 구분하는 것은 어렵다.

16. 동 물

animal
동물, 짐승
[ǽnəməl]

animal   animal   animal

ant
개미
[ænt]

ant   ant   ant   ant

bear(1)
곰
[bɛər]

bear   bear   bear

bird
새
[bəːrd]

bird   bird   bird   bird

---

animal	[애니멀]	A bear is a big animal.	곰은 몸집이 큰 동물이에요.
ant	[앤트]	The ants are diligent.	개미들은 부지런하다.
bear	[베어-ㄹ]	Bears like honey.	곰은 꿀을 좋아해.
bird	[버얼드]	Birds fly in the air.	새들은 공중을 날아다녀요.

cat 고양이 [kæt]	cat cat cat cat	
chicken 닭 [tʃikən]	chicken chicken chicken	
cow 암소, 젖소 [kau]	cow cow cow cow cow	
deer 사슴 [diər]	deer deer deer	
dog 개 [dɔːg]	dog dog dog dog dog	

cat	[캣]	I'm afraid of cats.	저는 고양이가 무서워요.
chicken	[취킨]	The chickens make a lot of noise.	닭들이 너무나 시끄럽게 해요.
cow	[카우]	Cows make milk."	암소들은 우유를 만들어요.
deer	[디얼]	Have you ever seen a deer?	사슴을 본 적이 있니?
dog	[더-ㄱ]	How many dogs are in the playground?	운동장에 개가 몇 마리나 있나요?

duck 오리 [dʌk]	duck duck duck duck
eagle 독수리 [iögl]	eagle eagle eagle eagle
elephant 코끼리 [éləfənt]	elephant elephant 
fish 물고기 [fiʃ]	fish fish fish fish 
fox 여우 [fɑks]	fox fox fox fox fox fox

duck	[덕]	The ducks can't fly.	오리는 날 수 없다.
eagle	[이-글]	The eagle expanded its wings.	독수리가 날개를 폈다.
elephant	[엘러풔ㄴ트]	The elephants are very strong.	코끼리는 매우 힘이 세다.
fish	[퓌쉬]	Did you catch any fish?	고기 좀 잡으셨어요?
fox	[팍스]	A fox is a wild animal.	여우는 야생 동물이다.

| **hawk** 매 [hɔ́ːk] | hawk hawk hawk hawk |

| **hen** 암탉 [hen] | hen hen hen hen |

| **horse** 말 [hɔːrs] | horse horse horse |

| **lion** 사자 [láiən] | lion lion lion lion lion |

| **monkey** 원숭이 [mʌ́ŋki] | monkey monkey |

hawk	[호-크]	The hawk circled round in the sky.	매는 하늘을 빙빙 돌았다.
hen	[헨]	Hen lays an egg.	암탉은 계란을 낳아요.
horse	[호올스]	Riding a horse is very funny.	말타는 건 재밌어요.
lion	[라이언]	A lion found a zebra.	사자가 얼룩말을 발견했어요.
monkey	[멍끼]	Monkeys like bananas.	원숭이들은 바나나를 좋아해요.

mouse 생쥐 [máus]	mouse mouse mouse
pig 돼지 [pig]	pig pig pig pig pig 
sheep 양 [ʃiːp]	sheep sheep sheep sheep
tiger 호랑이 [táigər]	tiger tiger tiger 
zoo 동물원 [zuː]	zoo zoo zoo zoo zoo zoo

mouse	[마우스]	Mice like chees.	쥐들은 치즈를 좋아한다.
pig	[픽]	Pigs eat a lot.	돼지는 많이 먹어요.
sheep	[쉽]	I have never seen sheep.	나는 양을 본 적이 없어요.
tiger	[타이걸]	Have you ever seen a tiger?	너는 호랑이를 본 적 있니?
zoo	[주-]	Let's go to the zoo.	동물원에 가자.

17. 우주와 자연

air
공기
[ɛər]

air air air air air

beach
물가, 바닷가
[biːtʃ]

beach beach beach beach

cloud
구름
[klaud]

cloud cloud cloud

earth
지구, 땅
[əːrθ]

earth earth earth earth

air	[에어ㄹ]	We would die without air.	우리는 공기가 없으면 죽고 말 거야.
beach	[비-잇취]	We will go to beach.	나는 올 여름 바닷가에 가고 싶어요.
cloud	[클라우드]	The birds fly over the clouds.	새들이 구름 위로 날아다녀요.
earth	[어-ㄹ쓰]	There are a lot of animals on the earth.	지구에는 많은 동물들이 있어요.

field
들판
[fiːld]

field field field field

grass
풀
[græs]

grass grass grass grass

gold
금
[gould]

gold gold gold gold

ground
땅, 운동장
[graund]

ground ground

hill
언덕
[hil]

hill hill hill hill hill hill

field	[퓌-ㄹ드]	The farmer works in the field.	농부가 들판에서 일을 해요.
grass	[그뢰쓰]	"Keep off the grass."	잔디에 들어가지 마시오.
gold	[고울드]	This box is full of gold.	이 상자는 금으로 가득 차 있어요.
ground	[그롸운드]	Let's play at the ground.	운동장에서 놀자.
hill	[힐]	A cottage is on a hill.	언덕 위에 작은집이 하나 있다.

ice
얼음
[ais]

ice　ice　ice　ice　ice　ice

island
섬
[áilənd]

island　island　island

jungle
밀림, 정글
[dʒʌ́ŋgl]

jungle jungle jungle jungle

lake
호수
[leik]

lake　lake　lake　lake

land
땅, 육지
[lænd]

land　land　land　land

ice	[아이스]	I slipped on the ice.	나는 얼음판에서 넘어졌어요.
island	[아일런드]	I have never been to the island.	나는 그 섬에 가본 적이 없어요.
jungle	[줘으글]	The lion is king of the jungle.	사자는 밀림의 왕이에요.
lake	[레익]	There are many lakes in Canada.	캐나다에는 호수가 많아요.
land	[랜드]	I traveld over land and sea last year.	나는 작년에 육지와 바다를 여행했다.

leaf	leaf leaf leaf leaf leaf leaf
나뭇잎	
[liːf]	

mountain	mountain mountain
산	
[mauntən]	

nature	nature nature nature
자연	
[néitʃər]	

plant	plant plant plant plant
식물	
[plænt]	

pool	pool pool pool pool pool
웅덩이, 연못	
[puːl]	

---

leaf	[리-프]	Look! The red leaf is falling.	봐봐! 빨간 나뭇잎이 떨어지고 있어.
mountain	[마운튼]	I climbed a mountain last Saturday.	나는 지난 토요일 산에 올랐어요.
nature	[네이쳐]	Nature is the best medicine	자연은 최고의 약이에요
plant	[플랜트]	The plants need water.	식물은 물이 필요하다.
pool	[푸-울]	Fish are in the pool.	연못에 물고기들이 있어요.

rain
비, 비가오다
[rein]

rain rain rain rain

rainbow
무지개
[ré inbóu]

rainbow rainbow rainbow

river
강
[rívər]

river river river

sand
모래
[sænd]

sand sand sand sand

sea
바다
[siː]

sea sea sea sea

rain	[뢰인]	I walked in the rain.	나는 빗속을 걸었어요.
rainbow	[뢰인보우]	we can see a rainbow after it rains.	비가 오고 난 후에는 무지개를 볼 수 있다.
river	[뤼버-ㄹ]	I jumped into the river.	나는 강에 뛰어 들었어요.
sand	[쌘드]	We built sand castles.	우리는 모래성을 쌓았다.
sea	[씨-]	I went to the sea last summer.	나는 지난 여름에 바다에 갔어요.

snow
눈, 눈이오다
[snou]

space
공간, 우주
[speis]

sun
태양, 햇빛
[sʌn]

water
물
[wɔ́ːtər]

wind
바람
[wind]

snow	[스노우]	It is snowing.	눈이 오고 있다.
space	[스뻬어스]	The people are looking for a parking space.	사람들이 주차할 공간을 찾고 있다.
sun	[썬]	The sun rises in the east.	해는 동쪽에서 뜬다.
water	[워-터]	People drink water every day.	사람들은 물을 매일 마신다.
wind	[윈드]	The paper is swing in the wind.	그 종이가 바람에 흔들린다.

18. 돈과 은행

bank
은행
[bǽŋk]

bank　bank　bank　bank

bank book
은행통장
[bǽŋk búk]

bank book　　bank book

bill
지폐
[bil]

bill　bill　bill　bill　bill　bill

cash
현금
[kǽʃ]

cash　cash　cash　cash

bank	[뱅크]	The bank opens at ten o'clock on the dot.	그 은행은 10시 정각에 문을 엽니다.
bank book	[뱅크 북]	I got my bankbook stolen.	예금통장을 잃어버렸어요.
bill	[빌]	I'll pay for the bill.	계산은 제가 할게요.
cash	[캐쉬]	I want to pay cash.	현금으로 계산을 하겠습니다.

check
수표

[tʃék]

check　check　check

coin
동전

[kɔin]

coin　coin　coin　coin　coin

credit card
신용카드

[krédit káːrd]

credit card　credit card

dollar
달러ㄹ

[dálər]

dollar　dollar　dollar　dollar

money
돈

[mʌ́ni]

money　money　money

check	[첵]	May I have the check, please?	계산서를 부탁합니다
coin	[코인]	Put the coins into that machine.	저 기계에 동전을 집어넣으세요.
credit card	[크레딧 카-드]	May I pay for it with a credit card?	신용카드로 지불해도 되나요?
dollar	[달러ㄹ]	It's ten dollars.	10달러입니다.
money	[머니]	How much money do you have?	넌 돈이 얼마 있니?

pay
지불하다
[pei]

pay　pay　pay　pay　pay

shop
가게
[ʃap]

shop　shop　shop　shop

store
가게, 상점
[stɔːr]

store　store　store

supermarket
슈퍼마켓
[súːpərmáːrkit]

supermatket　supermatket

safe
금고
[séif]

safe　safe　safe　safe

pay	[페이]	We pay the school expenses.	우리는 학비를 낸다.
shop	[샵]	I went to the toy shop.	나는 장난감가게로 갔다.
store	[스또어-르]	I came by a fruit store.	나는 과일 가게에 들렀다.
supermarket	[수-퍼르말킷]	I went to a supermarket to buy corn.	나는 옥수수를 사기 위해 슈퍼마켓에 갔다.
safe	[세이프]	Please place your valuables in this safe.	귀중품은 이 금고에 보관해 주세요.

19. 운동과 취미

art 미술, 예술
[ɑːrt]

art art art art art art

ball 공
[bɔːl]

ball ball ball ball ball ball

baseball 야구
[béisbɔ̀ːl]

baseball baseball

carnival 카니발
[káːrnəvəl]

carnival carnival

art	[알트]	My favorite subject is art.	내가 가장 좋아하는 과목은 미술이다.
ball	[버-얼]	This is my sister's ball.	이건 우리 누나의 공이예요.
baseball	[베이스볼]	It is a lot of fun to play baseball.	야구를 하는 것은 정말 재미있어.
carnival	[카-너블]	he Carnival is held every year for 46 days.	카니발은 매년 46일 동안 열립니다.

club	club club club club club
club 클럽, 동호회 [klʌb]	

| **concert**
콘서트
[kánsəːrt] | concert concert concert |

| **exercise**
운동, 연습
[éksərsáiz] | exercise exercise |

| **dance**
춤, 춤추다
[dæns] | dance dance dance |

| **design**
디자인
[dizain] | design design design |

club	[클럽]	He is my club friend.	그는 내 동호회 친구야.
concert	[컨서-트]	I'd like to go to a concert.	전 콘서트에 가고 싶어요.
exercise	[엑썰싸이즈]	It's important to exercise everyday.	매일 운동하는 것은 중요해요.
dance	[댄스]	I like to dance.	저는 춤추는 걸 좋아해요.
design	[디자인]	I don't like the design.	디자인이 마음에 들지 않습니다.

drum
북, 드럼

[drʌm]

drum   drum   drum   drum

game
게임

[geim]

game   game   game

golf
골프

[gɔ́lf]

golf   golf   golf   golf   golf

hiking
하이킹/도보여행

[háikiŋ]

hiking   hiking   hiking

movie
영화

[múːvi]

movie   movie   movie

drum	[드럼]	Peter is playing the drum.	Peter가 드럼을 치고 있어요.
game	[게임]	I like to play computer games.	컴퓨터 게임 하는 거 좋아해요.
golf	[골프]	He plays golf like a professional.	그는 마치 프로처럼 골프를 잘 친다.
hiking	[하이킹]	We'd go hiking together.	우린 자주 하이킹을 했죠
movie	[무-뷔]	I went to the movie with my friends.	나는 친구들과 영화를 보러 갔다.

music 음악 [mjúːzik]	music music music
photograph 사진 [fóutəɡræf]	photograph photograph
picture 그림 [píktʃər]	picture picture picture
sing 노래, 노래하다 [siŋ]	sing sing sing sing sing
skate 스케이트 [skeit]	skate skate skate skate

music [뮤-직] I like listening to music. 나는 음악 듣는 것을 좋아한다.
photograph [포터그래프] Taking photographs is not allowed. 사진 촬영이 금지되어 있습니다.
picture [픽쳐-] Look at the pictures. 그림을 보세요.
sing [씽] My hobby is to sing songs. 내 취미는 노래 부르는 것이다.
skate [스케잇-트] Let's go skating! 스케이트 타러가자!

94

sking	sking sking sking sking
스키	
[skíːŋ]	

soccer	soccer soccer	
축구	
[sákər]	

song	song song song song
노래	
[sɔːŋ]	

sport	sport sport sport sport
스포츠	
[spɔːrt]	

swim	swim swim swim	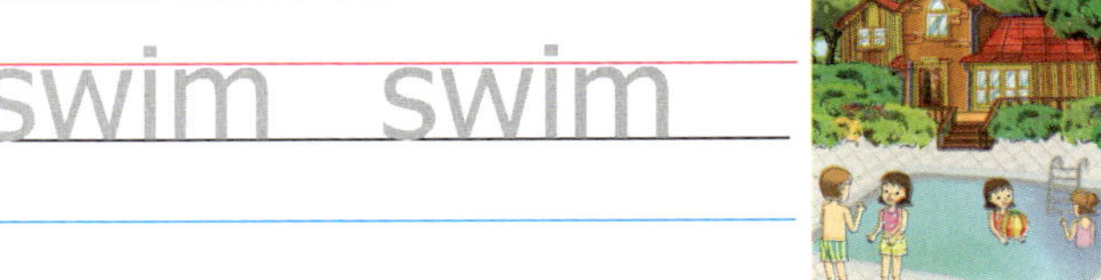
수영하다, 수영	
[swim]	

sking	[스키잉]	My family goes skiing every winter.	우리 가족은 겨울마다 스키를 탄다.
soccer	[싸커ㄹ]	I played soccer with my friends.	나는 친구들과 축구를 했어요.
song	[쏭]	I sang a song for my parents.	나는 부모님을 위해 노래를 불렀어요.
sport	[스포-올트]	Soccer is a popular sport in korea.	한국에서 축구는 인기가 좋다.
swim	[스윔]	We went swimming last Sunday.	지난 일요일 우리는 수영하러 갔다.

swing 그네 [swiŋ]	swing swing swing
tennis 테니스 [ténis]	tennis tennis tennis
video 비디오 [vídióú]	video video video 
violin 바이올린 [váiəlín]	violin violin violin 
xylophone 실로폰 [záiləfòun]	xylophone xylophone

---

swing [스윙] There are two boys on the swing. 그네에 남자아이 둘이 타고 있다.

tennis [테니스] She played tennis with her friend. 그녀는 친구와 함께 테니스를 쳤다.

video [브이디오] How often do you rent video tapes? 당신은 얼마나 자주 비디오 테이프를 빌려요?

violin [봐이얼린] I can play the violin. 저는 바이올린을 연주할 수 있어요.

xylophone [자일러포운] She is playing the xylophone. 그녀는 실로폰을 치고 있다.

20. 탈것들

airplane
비행기
[ɛərplén]

airplane airplane airplane

ambulance
구급차
[æmbjuləns]

ambulance ambulance

bicycle
자전거
[báisikəl]

bicycle bicycle

boat
보트, 작은배
[bout]

boat boat boat boat

airplane [에얼플레인]	I go to Busan by airplane.	나는 부산에 비행기로 간다.
ambulance [앰뷸런스]	The ambulance is arriving.	구급차가 도착하고 있다.
bicycle [바이시클]	Can you ride a bicycle?	자전거를 탈 수 있나요?
boat [보웃트]	My uncle has a big boat.	삼촌은 큰 보트를 가지고 계신다.

bus 버스 [bʌs]	bus bus bus bus bus
car 자동차 [kaːr]	car car car car 
ferry 유람선 [féri]	ferry ferry ferry ferry
motorcycle 오토바이 [móutərsáikl]	motorcycle motorcycle
ship 배 [ʃip]	ship ship ship ship

bus	[버스]	Look! Here comes a bus.	봐봐! 버스가 온다.
car	[카-ㄹ]	Let's get into this car.	이 차를 탑시다.
ferry	[페리-]	I want to take a ferry.	나는 유람선을 타고 싶어요.
motorcycle	[모우터-사이클]	She can drive a motorcycle.	그녀는 오토바이를 탈 수 있습니다.
ship	[쉽]	Look at that ship!	저 배를 봐요!

sled 썰매 [sled]	sled　sled　sled　sled　sled
subway 지하철 [sʌ́bwéi]	subway　　subway 
taxi 택시 [tǽksi]	taxi　taxi　taxi　taxi
train 기차 [trein]	train　train　train 
truck 트럭 [trʌk]	truck　truck　truck　truck

sled	[슬레드]	In winter, we sled.	겨울에 우리는 썰매를 탄다.
subway	[써브웨이]	We went to In-cheon by subway.	우리는 지하철로 인천에 갔다.
taxi	[택씨]	I took a taxi to the airport.	공항까지 택시를 타고 갔다.
train	[츄뤼인]	I will travel by train.	나는 기차로 여행할거예요.
truck	[츄럭]	The truck is big.	저 트럭은 크다.

21. 대립어

large 큰 [lɑːrdʒ]

large　large　large　large

thin 얇은 [θin]

thin　thin　thin　thin

fat 뚱뚱한 [fæt]

fat　fat　fat　fat　fat　fat

heavy 무거운 [hévi]

heavy　heavy　heavy

large	[라-ㄹ쥐]	I want large size skirt.	전 큰 사이즈 치마를 원해요.
thin	[띤]	This book is very thin.	이 책은 정말 얇아요.
fat	[퓌앳]	My cat is little fat, but very cute.	우리 고양이는 조금 뚱뚱하지만 귀여워요.
heavy	[헤뷔]	Elephants are really heavy.	코끼리는 아주 무겁다.

small
작은

[smɔːl]

small small small small

---

thick
두꺼운

[θik]

thick thick thick

---

thin
얇은

[θin]

thin thin thin thin thin

---

light(1)
가벼운

[lait]

light light light

---

small	[스모-ㄹ]	The ball is small.	그 공은 작다.
thick	[씩]	How thick is it?	그건 두께가 얼마나 되죠?
thin	[띤]	She is very thin.	그녀는 매우 날씬해요.
light	[라잇트]	Tom is lighter than his brother.	Tom은 그의 형보다 가벼워요.

| **quick**
빠른
[kwik] | quick quick quick |  |

| **sell**
팔다
[sel] | sell sell sell sell sell sell |

| **much**
많은
[mʌtʃ] | much much much much |

| **many**
많은
[méni] | many many many |  |

| **little**
작은
[lítl] | little little little little |

quick	[퀵]	He is quick to learn.	그는 배우는 속도가 빠르다.
sell	[쎌]	He sells cars.	그는 자동차를 판다.
much	[멋취]	Don't spend too much money.	돈을 너무 많이 쓰지 마세요.
many	[매니]	He has many friends.	그는 친구들이 많아요.
little	[리틀]	Tom is walking with the little boy.	Tom이 작은 소년과 걷고 있어요.

slow	slow　slow　slow	
느린		
[slou]		

buy	buy buy buy buy buy buy
사다, 구입하다	
[bai]	

little	little　little　little　little
약간의	
[lítl]	

few	few few few few few few
약간의	
[fjuː]	

big	big big big big big	
큰, 커다란		
[big]		

slow	[슬로우]	The turtle is slow.	거북이는 느리다.
buy	[바이]	I buy some chocolate at the store.	나는 가게에서 초콜릿을 삽니다.
little	[리를]	I have a little hope.	나에게는 약간의 희망이 있어.
few	[퓨-]	Tom has a few friends.	탐에게는 친구가 몇 명 있어.
big	[빅]	An elephant is a big animal.	코끼리는 몸집이 큰 동물이예요.

tall
키가 큰

[tɔːl]

tall tall tall tall tall

left
왼쪽, 왼쪽의

[left]

left left left left

down
아래로

[daun]

down down down down

under
~의 아래에

[ʌ́ndər]

under under under

young
젊은, 어린

[jʌŋ]

young young young young

tall	[토-ㄹ]	He is tall.	그는 키가 크다.
left	[레프트]	Turn left there.	저기서 왼쪽으로 도세요.
down	[다운]	I went down the stairs.	나는 계단을 내려갔어요.
under	[언덜]	There are ants under the tree.	나무 아래 개미들이 있어요.
young	[영]	He is young.	그는 어리다.

104

short
짧은, 키가작은

[ʃɔːrt]

short short short short

right
오른쪽

[rait]

right right right

up
위쪽으로

[ʌp]

up up up up up up

on
~의 위에

[an]

on on on on on on

old
늙은

[ould]

old old old old old old

short	[쇼-르트]	She is **shorter** than me.	그녀는 나보다 더 작아요.
right	[롸잇트]	Turn **right**.	오른쪽으로 도세요.
up	[엎]	Stand **up** please.	일어서 주세요.
on	[언]	My pencil is **on** the desk.	책상 위에 내 연필이 있어요.
old	[오울드]	How **old** are you?	몇 살이지요?

true 진실의 [trúː]		true true true true true
end 끝, 마치다 [end]		end end end end end
best 가장 좋은 [best]		best best best best 
come 오다 [kʌm]		come come come come
bright 밝은, 빛나는 [brait]		bright bright bright

true	[트루]	It is true.	사실이야.
end	[엔드]	This is the end.	이것으로 끝이다.
best	[베스트]	I did my best.	나는 최선을 다했어요.
come	[컴]	Grandfather will come next Friday.	할아버지는 다음주 금요일날 오실꺼에요.
bright	[브롸잇]	Look on the bright side of things.	밝은 면을 봐(긍정적으로 생각하렴).

false
거짓의
[fɔ́:ls]

false false false false

begin
시작하다
[bigín]

begin begin begin

worst
최악의
[wə́:rst]

worst worst worst worst

go
가다
[gou]

go go go go go

dark
어둠, 어두운
[da:rk]

dark dark dark dark

false	[폴스]	The rumor was false.	그 소문은 거짓이었어.
begin	[비긴]	Our class begins at 8.	수업은 8시에 시작한다.
worst	[워어ㄹ스트]	She was the worst singer.	그녀는 최악의 가수였어.
go	[고우]	I go to school everyday.	나는 매일 학교에 간다.
dark	[다아-ㄹ크]	My new skirt is dark blue.	저의 새 치마는 어두운 파란색이에요.

far	far far far far far

far
멀리
[fɑːr]

poor
가난한
[púər]

poor poor poor poor

start
출발하다
[stɑːrt]

start start start start

dirty
더러운, 불결한
[dɔ́ːrti]

dirty dirty dirty dirty dirty

in
~안에
[in]

in in in in in in

far	[파-ㄹ]	My house is far from here.	우리집은 여기서 멀어요.
poor	[푸얼]	She always helps the poor.	그녀는 항상 가난한 이들을 돕는다.
start	[스딸-ㅌ]	Let's start.	시작하자
dirty	[더-ㄹ리]	My brother's room is dirty all the time.	내 동생 방은 항상 더러워요.
in	[인]	There is a cat in the box.	상자 안에 고양이 한 마리가 있다.

near 가까운 [niər]	near near near near
rich 돈 많은 [ritʃ]	rich rich rich rich 
stop 멈추다 [stap]	stop stop stop stop
clean 깨끗한 [kliːn]	clean clean clean  
out 밖으로, 밖에 [aut]	out out out out out

near	[니얼]	Our house stands near my school.	우리집은 학교 옆에 있어요.
rich	[륏취]	He is very rich.	그는 매우 부유하다.
stop	[스땁]	He stopped to talk.	그는 이야기하기 위해 멈췄다.
clean	[클리인]	I clean my room everyday.	저는 제방을 매일 청소해요.
out	[아웃]	Let's go out.	우리 밖으로 나가자.

push
밀다

[puʃ]

strong
힘이 센, 강한

[strɔːŋ]

sit
앉다

[sit]

open
열다

[óupən]

glad
기쁜, 반가운

[glæd]

push	[푸쉬]	Push the door open.	문을 밀어서 열어요.
strong	[스트뤄-엉]	The boy looks strong.	그 소년은 강해 보인다.
sit	[씻]	Sit down, please.	앉아 주세요.
open	[오우쁜]	Open the door, please.	문좀 열어 주세요.
glad	[글래드]	I'm glad to meet you.	만나서 반가워.

pull				
당기다				
[pul]	pull	pull	pull	pull

weak				
약한				
[wíːk]	weak	weak	weak	weak

stand				
서다, 일어서다				
[stænd]	stand	stand	stand	stand

shut				
닫다, 덮다				
[ʃʌt]	shut	shut	shut	shut	shut

sad				
슬픈				
[sæd]	sad	sad	sad	sad

pull	[풀]	Pull the door open.	문을 당겨서 열어요.
weak	[위-크]	Tom is weak.	Tom은 (체력이)약해요.
stand	[스땐드]	Stand up, please.	일어서 주세요.
shut	[셧]	Please shut the window.	창문 좀 닫아 주세요.
sad	[쌔에드]	She looks sad.	그녀는 슬퍼보여.

high 높은 [hái]	high high high high
great 큰, 엄청난 [greit]	great great great great
wide 넓은 [waid]	wide wide wide 
fine 좋은 [fain]	fine fine fine fine fine fine
warm 따뜻한 [wɔːrm]	warm warm warm 

high	[하이]	Mt. Everest is really high.	에베레스트 산은 정말 높아요.
great	[그뤠잇]	I heard some great news!	나 엄청난 소식을 들었어!
wide	[와이드]	That place is wide.	그곳은 넓어요.
fine	[퐈인]	The weather is fine, today.	오늘 날씨가 좋아요.
warm	[워-ㄹ엄]	Today is warm.	오늘은 따뜻하다.

low 낮은 [lóu]	low low low low low	
little 작은 [lítl]	little little little little little	
narrow 좁은 [nǽrou]	narrow narrow narrow	
bad 나쁜 [bǽd]	bad bad bad bad	
cold 추운 [kóuld]	cold cold cold cold	

low	[로우]	The temperature is low today.	오늘은 기온이 낮다.
little	[리를]	You just look like a little kid.	넌 그냥 어린애처럼 보여.
narrow	[내로오우]	He jumped a narrow stream.	그는 좁은 개울을 뛰어넘었어.
bad	[베드]	I feel bad today.	난 오늘 기분이 나빠.
cold	[코울드]	It's cold in winter.	겨울은 추워요.

long
긴
[lɔːŋ]

long long long long

lot
많음
[lat]

lot lot lot lot lot lot

hate
싫어하다
[heit]

hate hate hate hate

hot
더운, 뜨거운
[hat]

hot hot hot hot hot hot

easy
쉬운
[íːzi]

easy easy easy easy

long	[러-엉]	A giraffe has a long neck.	기린은 목이 길어요.
lot	[랏]	There are a lot of people on the beach.	해변에 사람이 많아요.
hate	[헤잇트]	I hate mouse.	난 쥐를 싫어해.
hot	[핫]	I don't like hot weather.	나는 더운 날씨를 별로 안 좋아해요.
easy	[이-지]	It's easy to say "Thank you."	고맙다고 말하는 건 쉬워요.

short 짧은 [ʃɔ́ːrt]	short short short	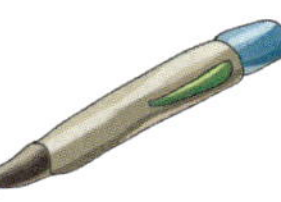
few 거의 없는 [fjúː]	few few few few few few	
like 좋아하다 [láik]	like like like like like	
cool 시원한 [kúːl]	cool cool cool cool	
difficult 어려운 [dífikʌ̀lt]	difficult difficult difficult	

short	[쇼올트]	She likes to wear short skirt.	그녀는 짧은 치마 입는 것을 좋아해.
few	[퓨]	I have few books.	나는 책이 거의 없어.
like	[라익]	Sally likes you.	셀리가 널 좋아해.
cool	[쿠울]	I want to drink cool water.	나 시원한 물이 마시고 싶어.
difficult	[디퓌컬트]	That is so difficult problem to solve.	저건 풀기에 너무 어려운 문제야.

115

behind 시작하다 [biháind]	behind behind behind
into ~안으로 [intu]	into into into into into into
happy 행복한 [hǽpi]	happy happy happy 
equal 같은 [íːkwəl]	equal equal equal equal

behind [비하인드] Tom smiles **behind** Merry. 수업은 8시에 시작한다.

into [인투] Jim went **into** his house. Jim은 그의 집으로 들어갔어요.

happy [해삐] I'm **happy** to be with you. 너랑 있어 행복해.

equal [이쿠얼] Ducks are **equal** in size. 오리들은 크기가 같다.

ahead
앞쪽에

[əhéd]

ahead　　ahead　　ahead

outside
밖에

[áutsáid]

outside　　　outside

unhappy
불행한

[ʌ̀nhǽpi]

unhappy　　unhappy

different
다른

[dífərənt]

different　　different

ahead	[어헤드]	She went ahead of me.	그녀는 나를 앞서갔다.
outside	[아웃사이드]	It's a lovely day outside.	밖에 날씨가 너무 좋아요.
unhappy	[언해삐]	She was unhappy about the news.	그녀는 그 소식에 슬픈 생각이 들었다.
different	[디퍼런트]	I need a different pen.	나 다른 펜이 필요해.

deep
깊은
[diːp]

deep   deep   deep

take
받다
[teik]

take take take take take

fast
빠른
[fæst]

fast   fast   fast   fast

cheap
값이 싼, 싸게
[tʃiːp]

cheap cheap cheap cheap

deep	[디-입]	How deep is the river?	강이 얼마나 깊나요?
take	[테익]	Take this letter to your mother.	이 편지를 어머니께 가져다 드리렴.
fast	[푸ㅔ스트]	It is very fast train.	이건 굉장히 빠른 기차예요.
cheap	[취-입]	The candy was very cheap.	그 사탕은 값이 쌌어요.

low
얕은
[lóu]

low low low low low low

give
주다
[gív]

give give give

slow
느린
[slóu]

slow slow slow slow slow

expensive
비싼
[ikspénsiv]

expensive expensive

low	[로우]	The stream was so low that we could cross it.	개울가가 얕아서 우리가 건널 수 있었다.
give	[기브]	Please, give me that book.	그 책을 좀 줘.
slow	[슬로우]	Will you slow down?	좀 천천히 할래?
expensive	[익스펜시브]	Isn't this pretty expensive?	이거 꽤 비싸지 않아?

22. 동사

act
행동하다
[ækt]

act act act act act act

am
be의 1인칭 단수 현재형
[æm]

am am am am am am

appear
나타나다
[əpíər]

appear appear appear

are
be의 2인칭 단수 현재형
[áːr]

are are are are are are

act	[액트]	He acts like a father.	그는 아빠인 것처럼 행동한다.
am	[앰]	I am no match for him.	나는 결코 그의 적수가 아니다.
appear	[어피얼]	He appears in the room.	그가 방에 나타났다(들어왔다).
are	[아-르]	Trees are very important for us.	나무는 우리에게 매우 중요합니다.

arrive
도착하다
[əráiv]

arrive arrive arrive

ask
물어보다
[æsk]

ask ask ask ask ask ask

be
~이다 ~이 있다
[biː]

be be be be be be

bear(2)
낳다
[bɛər]

bear bear bear bear

become
~이 되다
[bikʌ́m]

become become become

---

arrive	[어롸이브]	Dad will arrive soon.	도착하실꺼야.
ask	[애스크]	I asked myself.	나는 내 자신에게 물었습니다.
be	[비-]	Be a kind kid!	친절한 어린이가 되라!
bear	[베어-ㄹ]	Dogs usually bear four puppies.	개는 보통 4마리의 새끼를 낳는다.
become	[비큄]	Hungbu became the rich man.	흥부는 부자가 되었어요.

121

blow 불다 [blou]	blow blow blow blow blow
break 부수다 [breik]	break break break break
bring 가져오다 [briŋ]	bring bring bring 
broke 깨트렸다 [brouk]	broke broke broke broke
build 세우다, 짓다 [bild]	build build build build

blow [블로우]	My father is blowing up balloons.	아빠가 풍선을 불고 계셔요.
break [브뢰익크]	A glass is easy to break.	유리는 깨지기 쉽다.
bring [브륑]	Bring me the book, please.	그 책 좀 가져다 주렴.
broke [브로-크]	I broke my grandma's glasses.	내가 할머니의 안경을 깨뜨렸다.
build [빌드]	I want to build a doghouse.	나는 개집을 짓고 싶어요.

burn
타다, 태우다
[bəːɾn]

burn   burn   burn   burn

buy
사다
[bai]

buy   buy   buy   buy

call
부르다
[kɔːl]

call   call   call   call

carry
운반하다
[kǽri]

carry   carry   carry   carry

catch
잡다, 받다
[kætʃ]

catch   catch   catch   catch

burn	[버-ㄹ언]	Mom **burned** the steaks today.	엄마는 오늘 스테이크를 태웠어요.
buy	[바이]	Money cannot **buy** happiness.	돈으로는 행복을 살 수 없습니다.
call	[커얼]	My friends **call** me Sunny.	친구들은 저를 Sunny라고 불러요.
carry	[캐뤼]	I always **carry** schoolbag.	저는 항상 책가방을 가지고 다녀요.
catch	[캣취]	Cats are very good at **catching** mice.	고양이는 쥐를 아주 잘 잡아요.

change
바꾸다
[tʃeinʒ]

change　change　change

climb
오르다
[klaim]

climb　climb　climb　climb

close
닫다
[klouz]

close　close　close　close

come
오다
[kʌm]

come　come　come　come

could
can의 과거형
[kud]

could　could　could　could

change	[췌인지]	Don't Be Afraid of New Changes.	새로운 변화를 두려워하지 마세요
climb	[크라임]	I climbed a mountain.	나는 등산을 했어요.
close	[클로우즈]	Close one eye and look at that.	한쪽 눈을 감고 저것을 봐봐.
come	[컴]	He came into the room.	그는 방으로 들어왔다
could	[쿠드]	I could carry the box.	나는 그 상자를 옮길 수 있었어요.

124

count 수를 세다 [kaunt]	count count count count
cross 가로지르다 [crɔːs]	cross cross cross cross
cry 소리치다, 울다 [krai]	cry cry cry cry 
cut 베다, 깎다 [kʌt]	cut cut cut cut cut
die 죽다 [dai]	die die die die die die

count	[카운트]	Let's count to 10! 1, 2, 3…	10까지 세어보자! 일, 이, 삼…
cross	[크뤄스]	Let's cross the street.	길을 건너자.
cry	[크롸이]	"Why are you crying?"	왜 울고 있니?
cut	[컷]	I had cut my finger.	나는 손가락을 베었다.
die	[다이]	That sick dog will die.	저 아픈 개는 죽을거야.

does
do의 3인칭 단수
[dʌz]

does　does　does　does

draw
끌다
[drɔː]

draw　draw　draw　draw

drink
마시다
[driŋk]

drink　drink　drink

drive
운전하다
[draiv]

drive　drive　drive

drop
떨어뜨리다
[drap]

drop　drop　drop　drop

does	[더즈]	He does not dare to do it.	그는 그럴 용기가 없다.
draw	[드로우]	It's trying to draw us out.	우리를 끌어내려고 해요
drink	[쥬륑크]	If you are thirsty, drink some water.	목이 마르면 물을 좀 마시세요.
drive	[드롸이브]	Can you drive a car?	차 운전할 줄 알아요?
drop	[드롸ㅂ]	"Don't drop the dishes."	접시 떨어뜨리지 마라.

eat 먹다 [iːt]	eat eat eat eat	
enjoy 즐기다 [éndʒɔ́i]	enjoy enjoy enjoy	
excite 흥분시키다 [iksáit]	excite excite excite excite	
excuse 용서하다 [ikskjúːz]	excuse excuse excuse	
feel 느끼다 [fiːl]	feel feel feel feel feel	

eat	[이-잇]	I like to eat salads.	샐러드는 먹는 걸 좋아해요.
enjoy	[엔줘이]	My dad enjoys driving.	아빠는 운전을 즐기셔요.
excite	[익씨이트]	The game excited us.	그 시합은 우리를 흥분시켰다.
cxcuse	[익스큐즈]	Excuse me.	실례합니다.
feel	[퓌-일]	I feel the summer is coming.	여름이 오고있는게 느껴져요.

fight 싸우다 [fait]	fight fight fight fight
fill 채우다 [fil]	fill fill fill fill fill 
follow 따르다 [fálou]	follow follow follow follow
find 찾다, 발견하다 [faind]	find find find find find
finish 끝내다, 마치다 [fíniʃ]	finish finish finish finish

fight	[퐈잇트]	Sometimes I fight with my brother.	가끔 동생이랑 싸워요.
fill	[퓔]	Fill in the blank.	빈칸을 채우세요.
follow	[퐈ㄹ로우]	"Where is the hospital?" "Follow me"	"병원이 어디있나요" "저를 따라 오세요"
find	[퐈인드]	I can't find my doll.	제 인형을 찾을 수가 없어요.
finish	[퓌니쉬]	Let's finish it today.	오늘 그걸 끝냅시다.

fix	fix fix fix fix fix fix
fix 수리하다 [fiks]	
fly 날다 [flai]	fly fly fly fly fly 
forget 잊다 [fərgét]	forget forget forget forget
get 얻다 [get]	get get get get get
give 주다 [giv]	give give give give

fix	[퓌ㄱ스]	Dad and I will fix the roof today.	아빠랑 오늘 지붕을 고칠꺼에요.
fly	[플롸이]	I can't fly.	나는 날 수 없어요.
forget	[폴겟]	Did you forget to buy some apples?	사과 사는 거 잊으셨어요?
get	[겟]	I got so many nice gifts.	난 멋진 선물들을 많이 받았어.
give	[기브]	He gave it to me.	그는 나에게 그것을 주었다.

go	[gou]	go go go go go go
grow	[grou]	grow grow grow grow
happen	[hǽpən]	happen happen happen
hate	[heit]	hate hate hate hate
have	[hæv]	have have have

go 가다

grow 자라다

happen 발생하다

hate 미워하다

have 가지고 있다

go	[고우]	Where are you going?	어디 가니?
grow	[그로우]	Most people want to grow taller.	대부분의 사람들은 키가 더 크길 바랍니다
happen	[해쁜]	How did it happen?	어떻게 그 일이 발생했나요?
hate	[헤이트]	They hate her deeply.	그들은 그녀를 몹시 미워한다.
have	[해브]	I have a lot of stamps.	저는 우표를 아주 많이 가지고 있어요.

hear 듣다 [hiər]		
help 돕다 [help]		
hide 숨기다, 숨다 [haid]		
hit 때리다 [hit]		
hold 잡다, 붙들다 [hould]		

hear	[히어-ㄹ]	I was very sad to hear the news.	나는 이 소식을 듣고 너무 슬펐어.
help	[헬-프]	Help me, please!	저를 도와주세요!
hide	[하이드]	Don't hide my doll.	내 인형 숨기지마!!
hit	[힛]	Don't hit me!	나를 때리지 마.
hold	[호울드]	"Hold my hand!", he cries.	"내 손을 잡아!" 그가 외쳤어요.

hope 바라다 [houp]	hope hope hope hope
hurry 서두르다 [həːri]	hurry hurry hurry hurry
hurt 다치게 하다 [həːrt]	hurt hurt hurt hurt hurt
is be의 3인칭 단수 현재형 [iz]	is is is is is is
join 참가하다 [dʒɔin]	join join join join join

hope	[호웁]	I hope you have a good time.	좋은 시간되시길 바랍니다.
hurry	[허-뤼]	Hurry up, or we'll be late.	서둘러! 안 그러면 늦을꺼야.
hurt	[허-르트]	I am badly hurt.	난 심하게 다쳤어요.
is	[이즈]	Milk is good for your health.	우유는 건강에 좋습니다
join	[조인]	Korea also joined the event.	한국도 그 행사에 참여했습니다

jump 뛰어오르다 [dʒʌmp]	jump　jump　jump　jump
keep 계속하다 [kiːp]	keep　keep　keep　keep
kick 차다 [kik]	kick　kick　kick　kick 
kill 죽이다, 없애다 [kil]	kill　kill　kill　kill　kill　kill
knock 두드리다 [nak]	knock　knock　knock 

jump	[쥐ㅁ프]	Teddy is ready to jump up.	Teddy는 뛰어오를 준비가 되었어요
keep	[키-입]	Keep your room clean.	당신의 방을 깨끗히 유지하세요.
kick	[킥]	Tom kicked a ball.	Tom은 공을 찼어요.
kill	[킬]	Cats kill the mouse.	고양이는 쥐를 죽여요.
knock	[낙]	I knocked the door.	전 노크를 했어요.

know
알다, 이해하다
[nou]

know know know know

jump
뛰어오르다
[dʒʌmp]

jump jump jump

laugh
웃다
[læf]

laugh laugh laugh laugh

lead
이끌다
[liːd]

lead lead lead lead

learn
배우다
[ləːrn]

learn learn learn learn

know	[노우]	Do you know what I mean?	내가 무슨 말 하는 지 알겠어?
jump	[줘ㅁ프]	Teddy is ready to jump up.	Teddy는 뛰어오를 준비가 되었어요
laugh	[래프]	He laughs loudly.	그는 큰 소리로 웃었어요.
lead	[리-드]	Hope can lead to miracles.	희망은 기적을 이끈다.
learn	[러-언]	It takes time to learn how to ski.	스키를 배우는 데는 시간이 걸려.

leave
떠나다
[liːv]

leave   leave   leave

let
시키다
[let]

let   let   let   let   let   let

lie
눕다
[lai]

lie   lie   lie   lie   lie   lie

like
좋아하다
[laik]

like   like   like   like   like

live
살다
[liv]

live   live   live   live

leave	[리-브]	I leave at 3.	나는 3시에 떠나요.
let	[렛]	I let him go out.	그를 나가게 했어요.
lie	[라이]	I lay down on the grass.	저는 풀 밭에 누웠습니다.
like	[라이크]	I like dancing.	저는 춤추는 걸 좋아해요.
live	[리브]	You cannot live alone.	여러분은 혼자 살 수 없습니다.

look		
look 보다 [luk]	look look look	

look look look

lose 잃다 [luːz]

lose lose lose lose

love 사랑하다 [lʌv]

love love love love love

make 만들다 [meik]

make make make make

marry 결혼하다 [mǽri]

marry marry marry

look	[룩]	Look at it. Do you know what it is?	이것 좀 봐. 이게 뭔지 알어?
lose	[루-즈]	He lost his room key.	그는 자기 방 열쇠를 잃어버렸다.
love	[러브]	Mom and dad love each other.	엄마 아빠는 서로를 사랑하셔요.
make	[메이크]	I made a cake for my mother.	나는 어머니를 위해 케이크를 만들었어요.
marry	[메리]	I'm getting married next month	전 다음 달에 결혼해요.

may
~해도 좋다
[mei]

may may may may

meet
만나다
[miːt]

meet meet meet

move
움직이다
[muːv]

move move move move

must
꼭 해야만 한다
[mʌst]

must must must must

need
필요로 하다
[niːd]

need need need need

may	[메이]	You **may** go now.	넌 이제 가도 좋다.
meet	[미잇트]	I am glad to **meet** you.	만나게 되어서 기뻐요.
move	[무-브]	We **moved** to a new house.	우리는 새집으로 이사했어요.
must	[머스트]	You **must** do this.	당신은 이것을 해야만 한다.
need	[니-드]	I **need** money.	나는 돈이 필요하다.

open
열다
[óupən]

open open open open

pass
지나가다
[pæs]

pass pass pass pass

pay
돈을 치르다
[pei]

pay pay pay pay

pick
따다
[pik]

pick pick pick pick pick

play
연주하다, 놀다
[plei]

play play play play

open	[오우픈]	I didn't open the window.	내가 창문을 열지 않았다.
pass	[패스]	I passed through the park.	나는 공원을 가로질러 지나갔다.
pay	[페이]	I'll pay next time.	다음 번에는 제가 낼게요.
pick	[픽]	Please, pick one of them.	그것들 중 하나를 고르세요.
play	[플레이]	She plays the violin very well.	그녀는 바이올린 연주를 매우 잘한다.

| **please** 기쁘게 하다 [pliːz] | please please please |  |

| **pull** 끌다, 당기다 [pul] | pull   pull   pull   pull   pull |

| **push** 밀다 [puʃ] | push   push   push   push |

| **put** 놓다, 두다 [put] | put   put   put   put   put |

| **ran** 달렸다 [ræn] | ran   ran   ran   ran   ran |

please	[플리이즈]	I am pleased to see you.	너를 보게 되어 기뻐.
pull	[풀]	He pulled my hair.	그가 내 머리를 잡아 당겨요.
push	[푸쉬]	Don't push friends.	친구를 밀지 마세요.
put	[풋]	I put some flowers into the vase.	꽃병에 꽃 몇 송이를 넣었다.
ran	[뤈]	Tiger ran fast.	호랑이는 빨리 달렸다.

read	read read read read
읽다	
[riːd]	

record	record record record
기록하다	
[rikɔ́ːrd]	

remember	remember remember
기억하다	
[rimémbər]	

return	return return return
돌아오다	
[ritə́rn]	

ride	ride ride ride ride ride
타다	
[raid]	

read	[리-드]	They **read** e-books.	그들은 전자책을 읽습니다.
record	[뢰커-르드]	I **record** everything in this note.	나는 모든 것을 이 노트에 기록한다.
remember	[뤼멤버얼]	I **remember** her.	나는 그녀를 기억한다.
return	[리터-언]	The couple **returned** to Korea.	이 커플은 한국으로 돌아왔다.
ride	[롸이드]	Can you **ride** a bicycle?	자전거 탈 줄 아니?

ring 울리다 [riŋ]	ring ring ring ring ring
run 달리다 [rʌn]	run run run run run
say 말하다 [sei]	say say say say say say
see 보다 [siː]	see see see see 
sell 보내다 [sel]	sell sell sell sell sell

ring	[륑]	The telephone is ringing.	전화가 울리고 있어요.
run	[뤄ㄴ]	I like to run.	나는 달리는 걸 좋아해요.
say	[쎄이]	Don't say bad words!	나쁜 말을 하지 마세요!
see	[씨-]	I want to see you!	네가 보고싶어!
sell	[셀]	He sells books, pencils and all that.	그는 책, 연필 등을 판다.

send 보내다 [send]	send send send send
set 놓다 [set]	set set set set set set
shall ~일 것이다 [ʃæl]	shall shall shall shall
shoot 쏘다, 던지다 [ʃuːt]	shoot shoot shoot shoot
shout 소리치다 [ʃaut]	shout shout shout shout

send	[쎈드]	I will send you an e-mail.	나는 너에게 e-mail을 보낼 것이다.
set	[세트]	He set a new world record.	그는 세계 신기록을 세웠습니다.
shall	[쉘]	I shall be very happy to see you.	너를 보게 되면 매우 기쁠 거야.
shoot	[슛]	He tried to shoot a bird.	그는 새 한 마리를 쏘려고 하였다.
shout	[샤웃]	Don't shout to your brother.	동생에게 소리치지 마라.

show 보이다 [ʃou]	show show show show
sing 노래하다 [siŋ]	sing sing sing sing
sit 앉다 [sit]	sit sit sit sit sit sit
slide 미끄러지다 [slaid]	slide slide slide slide slide
smell 냄새맡다 [smel]	smell smell smell smell

show	[쇼우]	Can you show it to me? · 그것을 내게 보여줄 수 있니?
sing	[씽]	She sang a song merrily. · 그녀는 유쾌하게 노래를 불렀다.
sit	[씨트]	We sat face to face. · 우리는 마주 보고 앉았다.
slide	[슬라이드]	She slid on the ice. · 그녀는 얼음판 위에서 미끄러졌다.
smell	[스멜]	It smells good. · 좋은 냄새가 난다.

smile	smile smile smile
웃다, 미소지다	
[smail]	

speak
말하다
[spiːk]

speak   speak   speak

spell
철자하다
[spel]

spell   spell   spell   spell

spend
낭비하다
[spend]

spend spend spend spend

stand
서다
[stænd]

stand stand stand stand

---

smile	[스마일]	She **smiled** at me.	그녀가 나를 보고 웃었다.
speak	[스피-크]	They don't **speak** Korean very well.	그들은 한국말을 잘하지 못해.
spell	[스펠]	The word is wrongly **spelled**.	그 단어는 철자가 잘못되어 있다.
spend	[스뺀드]	How much money do you **spend**?	돈을 얼마나 썼니?
stand	[스탠드]	Please **stand** up.	일어서 주시기 바랍니다

start	[스타-트]	The bus started on time.	버스는 정각에 출발했다.
stay	[스테이]	I stayed home all day long today.	나는 오늘 하루 종일 집에 있었어.
stop	[스탑]	You'd better stop smoking.	당신은 담배를 끊는 것이 좋겠어요.
strike	[스뜨롸익]	I strike a ball.	나는 공을 친다.
study	[스타디]	They study hard all day long.	그들은 하루 종일 열심히 공부합니다.

surprise 놀라게하다 [sərpráiz]	surprise surprise
swim 수영하다 [swim]	swim swim swim swim
take 잡다 [teik]	take take take take
talk 이야기하다 [tɔ:k]	talk talk talk talk
taste 맛을 보다 [teist]	taste taste taste taste

surprise	[써프라이즈]	I was very surprised at the news.	나는 그 소식을 듣고 매우 놀랐다.
swim	[스윔]	Do not swim in the sea!	바다에서 수영하지 마세요!
take	[테이크]	I was taken ill.	병에 걸렸다.
talk	[토-크]	I often talk to my mom.	난 가끔 엄마와 얘기를 해.
taste	[테이스트]	It tastes sweet.	단맛이 난다.

teach	teach teach teach teach
teach 가르치다 [tiːtʃ]	
tell 말하다 [tel]	tell tell tell tell tell tell
thank ~에게 감사하다 [θæŋk]	thank thank thank thank
think ~라고 생각하다 [θiŋk]	think think think think
throw 던지다 [θrou]	throw throw throw throw

teach	[티-취]	He teaches us English.	그는 우리에게 영어를 가르친다.
tell	[텔]	Now tell me the truth.	이제 진실을 말하시죠.
thank	[쌩크]	Thank you for helping me!	저를 도와주셔서 고맙습니다!
think	[씽크]	He is thinking something.	그는 무언가를 생각하고 있다.
throw	[쓰로우]	The pitcher threw a ball to me.	투수가 나에게 공을 던졌어요.

touch	touch touch touch touch
~을 만지다	
[tʌtʃ]	

understand	understand understand
이해하다	
[ʌndərstænd]	

use	use use use use use use
사용하다	
[juːz]	

wait	wait wait wait wait wait
기다리다	
[weit]	

wake	wake wake wake wake
깨다	
[weik]	

touch	[터취]	Never touch strange animals.	낯선 동물들을 만지지 마세요.
understand	[언더스탠드]	This is difficult to understand.	이것은 이해하기 어렵다.
use	[유-즈]	We use soap every day.	우리는 매일 비누를 사용합니다.
wait	[웨잇]	Min-ho is waiting for his girl friend.	민호는 그의 여자 친구를 기다립니다.
wake	[웨이크]	I will wake up early tomorrow.	내일 아침에는 일찍 일어날 거야.

walk

walk
걷다, 산책하다
[wɔːk]

walk   walk   walk

want

want
원하다
[wɑnt]

want   want   want   want

was

was
am, is의 과거형
[wɑz]

was   was   was   was

wear

wear
입고 있다
[wɛər]

wear   wear   wear   wear

went

went
갔다
[went]

went   went   went   went

walk	[워-억]	I walk in the park with my wife everyday.	나는 매일 아내와 공원을 걷는다.
want	[원트]	Everyone wants to be happy.	모든 사람들이 행복하기를 원한다.
was	[워즈]	I was very angry.	나는 매우 화가 났습니다.
wear	[웨어]	He likes to wear suits.	그는 정장 입는 것을 좋아합니다.
went	[웬트]	We went to an ice rink.	우리는 스케이트장에 갔어.

were are의 과거형 [wəːr]	were were were were
will ~일 것이다 [wíl]	will will will will will will
win 이기다 [win]	win win win win win win
wonder 이상하게 여기다 [wʌ́ndər]	wonder wonder wonder
write 쓰다,편지를 쓰다 [rair]	write write write write

were	[워-ㄹ]	You **were** my best friend!	너는 내게 가장 좋은 친구였어!
will	[윌]	I **will** play online games.	나는 온라인 게임을 할 거야.
win	[윈]	We should **win** this game.	우린 이 경기를 이겨야 합니다.
wonder	[원더]	I **wonder** about that.	나는 그것을 이상하게 생각하고 있다.
write	[롸이트]	**Write** a letter to your parents.	부모님께 편지를 쓰세요

150

23. 형용사

able ~할 수 있는 [éibl]	able able able able
absent 결석한 [ǽbsənt]	absent absent absent
all 모든, 모두 [ɔːl]	all all all all all all
another 또 하나의 [ənʌ́ðər]	another another another

able	[에이블]	I am able to run very fast.	나는 매우 빨리 달릴 수 있습니다.
absent	[엡선트]	I was absent from school.	나는 학교에 결석했어요.
all	[올]	I wanted to buy them all!	난 책을 모두 사고 싶었어!
another	[어나더]	I have another plan.	난 다른 계획이 있어.

asleep
잠든

[əslíːp]

asleep asleep asleep

awake
깨어 있는

[əwéik]

awake awake awake

bad
나쁜, 심한

[bæd]

bad bad bad bad

best
가장 좋은, 최고의

[best]

best best best best

big
큰

[big]

big big big big big big

asleep	[어스립-]	The boys are asleep.	아이들은 잠들었어요
awake	[어웨이크]	I was awake all the night.	나는 밤새도록 깨어 있었다.
bad	[베드]	It can be bad for your health.	그것은 여러분의 건강에 나쁩니다.
best	[베스트]	Dogs are man's best friend.	개는 인간의 가장 좋은 친구입니다.
big	[빅]	China is a big country.	중국은 큰 나라입니다.

brave 용감한 [breiv]	brave brave brave brave
bright 밝은, 빛나는 [brait]	bright bright bright
certain 확실한 [sə́ːrtin]	certain certain certain
cheap 값이 싼 [tʃiːp]	cheap cheap cheap
clean 청결한,깨끗한 [kliːn]	clean clean clean

brave	[브레이브]	They are strong and brave.	그들은 강하고 용감합니다.
bright	[브라이트]	It's very bright in the room.	방안이 매우 밝다.
certain	[써-튼]	It is certain that he told a lie.	그가 거짓말을 했음에 틀림없다.
cheap	[칩-]	This dress is cheap.	이 드레스는 저렴하다.
clean	[크린]	Always keep the kitchen clean.	항상 부엌을 깨끗하게 유지하세요.

clear
맑게 갠, 깨끗한
[kliər]

clear   clear   clear   clear

comic
희극의
[kámik]

comic   comic   comic

cute
귀여운
[kjuːt]

cute   cute   cute   cute

dark
어두운
[daːrk]

dark   dark   dark   dark

deep
깊은
[diːp]

deep   deep   deep

clear	[크리어]	The sky will clear up by Saturday.	토요일까지는 하늘이 맑게 갤 거야.
comic	[카믹]	He is a comic writer.	그는 희극 작가이다.
cute	[큐트]	Rabbits are very cute.	토끼는 매우 귀엽습니다.
dark	[다-크]	It began to grow dark.	날이 어두워지기 시작했다.
deep	[디-프]	Take a deep breath.	숨을 깊이 쉬세요

difficult
어려운, 곤란한

[dífikʌ́lt]

difficult difficult difficult

dirty
더러운

[də́ːrti]

dirty dirty dirty dirty

dry
마른, 건조한

[drai]

dry dry dry dry dry dry

early
이른

[ə́ːrli]

early early early early

easy
쉬운

[íːzi]

easy easy easy

---

difficult	[디피컬트]	Math is so boring and difficult!	수학은 너무 지루하고 어려워!
dirty	[더-ㄹ티]	I found the room dirty.	나는 방이 더럽다고 생각했다.
dry	[드라이]	The weather is very cold and dry.	날씨가 매우 춥고 건조하다.
early	[어-리]	I will wake up early tomorrow.	내일 아침에는 일찍 일어날 거야.
easy	[이-지]	It's not an easy task.	그것은 쉬운 일은 아니다.

elder 손위의 [éldər]	elder elder elder elder	
equal 같은, 동등한 [kwəl]	equal equal equal equal	
exact 정확한 [igzǽkt]	exact exact exact exact	
famous 유명한 [féiməs]	famous famous famous	
fast 빠른 [fæst]	fast fast fast fast	

elder	[엘더]	He is my elder brother.	그는 나의 형이다.
equal	[이-퀄]	Everyone is equal.	모든 사람은 동등하다.
exact	[이그제트]	Let's set an exact date!	정확한 날짜를 잡읍시다!
famous	[페이머스]	She is a famous politician.	그녀는 유명한 정치인 입니다.
fast	[페스트]	I always want to go faster.	저는 항상 빠르게 달리고 싶습니다.

fat 살찐 [fæt]	fat fat fat fat fat fat
fine 좋은, 훌륭한 [fain]	fine fine fine fine
funny 재미있는 [fʌ́ni]	funny funny funny funny
gentle 온화한, 친절한 [dʒéntl]	gentle gentle gentle
glad 기쁜, 즐거운 [glæd]	glad glad glad glad

fat	[펫]	Eating at night makes you fat.	밤에 먹으면 살이 찐다.
fine	[퐈인]	I hope it will be fine tomorrow.	내일 날이 맑으면 좋겠다.
funny	[퍼니]	They are very nice and funny.	그들은 아주 착하고 재미있어.
gentle	[젠틀]	He is good and gentle.	그는 착하고 친절한 사람입니다.
glad	[글래드]	I'm so glad to meet you.	만나서 정말 반갑습니다.

happy 행복한, 기쁜 [hǽpi]	happy happy happy
heavy 무거운 [hévi]	heavy heavy heavy
high 높은 [hai]	high high high high
hot 더운, 뜨거운 [hɑt]	hot hot hot hot hot hot
interesting 재미있는 [íntəristiŋ]	interesting interesting

happy	[해피]	Everyone wants to be happy.	모든 사람들이 행복하기를 바랍니다.
heavy	[헤비]	You're too heavy.	당신은 너무 무거워요.
high	[하이]	It is the highest mountain in the world.	그것은 세계에서 가장 높은 산입니다.
hot	[핫]	It was very hot today.	오늘은 날씨가 정말 더웠어.
interesting	[인터레스팅]	New York is an interesting city.	뉴욕은 흥미로운 도시입니다.

large 큰, 넓은 [lɑːrdʒ]	large large large large
last 최후의, 마지막의 [læst]	last last last last last
less ~보다 적은 [les]	less less less less
light 가벼운 [lait]	light light light light
little 작은, 조금 [lítl]	little little little little

단어	발음	예문	뜻
large	[라-쥐]	Mine is a large family.	우리 집은 대가족입니다.
last	[레스트]	It was really hot last week.	지난 주는 정말 더웠습니다.
less	[레스]	I am less healthy than I look.	나는 보이는 것만큼 건강하지 않다.
light	[라이트]	Let's have a light breakfast.	아침은 가볍게 먹읍시다.
little	[리틀]	I feel a little tired today.	나는 오늘 조금 피곤해.

long
긴, 오랫동안
[lɔːŋ]

long long long long

low
낮은, 낮게
[lou]

low low low low low

lucky
행운인,운이좋은
[ʌ́ki]

lucky lucky lucky lucky

main
주요한, 주된
[mein]

main main main main

many
많은, 다수의
[mέni]

many many many

long	[롱-]	Chile is a very long country.	칠레는 길이가 매우 긴 나라입니다.
low	[로우]	It is low in calories.	그것은 칼로리가 낮습니다.
lucky	[럭키]	You are a lucky guy.	당신은 운이 정말 좋은 사람이군요
main	[메인]	The North's main export is coal.	북한의 주요 수출품은 석탄이다.
many	[메니]	Many children love dogs.	많은 어린이들이 강아지를 좋아합니다.

more
더 많은
[mɔːr]

more　more　more　more

most
가장 많은
[moust]

most　most　most　most

much
많은, 다량의
[mʌtʃ]

much　much　much　much

narrow
좁은
[nǽrou]

narrow　narrow　narrow

near
근처의
[niər]

near　near　near　near

more	[모어-ㄹ]	He eats more fish than meat.	그는 고기보다 생선을 더 많이 먹는다
most	[모우스트]	China won the most gold medals.	중국은 가장 많은 금메달을 땄다.
much	[마취]	Too much salt is bad for you!	소금을 너무 많이 먹으면 건강에 해로워요!
narrow	[내로우]	He's narrow-minded.	그는 마음이 좁은 사람입니다.
near	[니어ㄹ]	Is there a pharmacy near here?	이 근처에 약국이 있나요?

old		
old 늙은, 낡은 [ould]	old old old old old old	

other		
other 다른,그 밖의 [ʌðər]	other other other other	

own		
own 자기 자신의 [oun]	own own own own	

pretty		
pretty 예쁜, 귀여운 [príti]	pretty pretty pretty	

proud		
proud 자랑스러운 [praud]	proud proud proud	

old	[올드]	He is considerate of old people.	그는 노인들에게 동정심이 많다.
other	[아더]	Do not push other children.	다른 어린이들을 밀지 마세요.
own	[오운]	I have my own logic.	나는 내 생각을 가지고 있어요.
pretty	[프리티]	They are so pretty!	그들은 너무 예뻐!
proud	[프라우드]	I am very proud of myself!	내 자신이 정말 자랑스러워!

162

quick 빠른 [kwik]	quick quick quick quick
real 진짜의, 진정한 [ríəl]	real real real real real
short 짧은 [ʃɔːrt]	short short short short
silent 조용한, 말없는 [sáilənt]	silent silent silent
simple 단순한, 간단한 [símpl]	simple simple simple

quick [퀵]	Be as quick as ever you can.	가능한 한 빨리 하세요.
real [리얼]	You are a real angel!	당신은 진정한 천사예요!
short [쇼-르트]	She is short and looks weak.	그녀는 키가 작고 약해 보여.
silent [싸일런트]	She remained silent.	그녀는 계속 침묵을 지켰다.
simple [심플]	It is very simple and easy.	그것은 매우 단순하고 쉽습니다.

slow
늦은, 느린
[slou]

slow　slow　slow　slow

small
작은, 소형의
[smɔːl]

small　small　small　small

soft
부드러운,유연한
[sɔft]

soft　soft　soft　soft

some
얼마간의
[sʌm]

some　some　some

special
특별한
[spéʃəl]

special　special　special

slow	[스로우]	You need to slow down.	좀 천천히 해 주세요.
small	[스모-ㄹ]	She is very small but healthy.	매우 작지만 건강하답니다.
soft	[소프트]	The hair was soft like silk.	그 털은 비단 같이 부드러웠다.
some	[썸]	Would you have some tea?	홍차를 드시겠습니까?
special	[스페셜]	Do you have any special plans?	특별한 계획이 있나요?

straight
곧은
[streit]

straight straight straight

strange
이상한
[streindʒ]

strange strange strange

strong
강한, 튼튼한
[strɔŋ]

strong strong strong

such
그러한
[sʌtʃ]

such such such such

sunny
양지 바른
[sʌ́ni]

sunny sunny sunny

---

straight [스트레이트] After work I go straight home.   저는 일이 끝나면 곧바로 집으로 갑니다.
strange [스트레인쥐] I had a strange dream.   나는 이상한 꿈을 꾸었어요.
strong [스트롱] He is strong and quick.   그는 힘이 세고 빠릅니다.
such [써취] It was such a beautiful place.   정말 아름다운 곳이었습니다.
sunny [써니] It was sunny.   날씨가 화창했다.

sure
확실한
[ʃuər]

sure　sure　sure　sure

sweet
단, 감미로운
[swiːt]

sweet sweet sweet sweet

tall
키가 큰
[tɔːl]

tall tall tall tall tall tall

thick
두꺼운
[θik]

thick　thick　thick　thick

thin
얇은
[θin]

thin　thin　thin　thin

sure	[슈어]	He is sure of winning.	자기가 이긴다고 확신하고 있다.
sweet	[스위-트]	It is very sweet and cool.	그것은 매우 달콤하고 시원합니다.
tall	[토-ㄹ]	But she is taller than me!	하지만 나보다 키가 더 커!
thick	[씨크]	I hate to wear this thick coat.	나는 이 두꺼운 코트를 입는 것을 싫어한다.
thin	[씬]	The cloth has worn thin.	그 천은 낡아 얇아졌다.

thirsty 목마른 [θə́ːrsti]	thirsty thirsty thirsty	
tired 피곤한 [taiərd]	tired tired tired tired	
true 진실한 [truː]	true true true true	
used 익숙한 [juːst]	used used used used	
warm 따뜻한 [wɔːrm]	warm warm warm	

thirsty [써-스티]	I'm just not that thirsty.	목마르진 않아.
tired [타이어드]	I feel a little tired today.	나는 오늘 약간 피곤해.
true [트루-]	He is not your true friend.	그는 네 진정한 친구가 아니야.
used [유-스트]	They are used to danger.	그들은 위험에 익숙해 있다
warm [워-ㅁ]	The weather is getting warmer.	날씨가 점점 따뜻해지고 있습니다.

weak		weak weak weak weak
약한	[wiːk]	

welcome		welcome welcome
환영받는	[wélkəm]	

well		well well well well
잘, 건강한	[wel]	

wide		wide wide wide wide
넓은	[waid]	

weak	[위-크]	I have a weak stomach.	위장이 약합니다.
welcome	[웰컴]	You'll be made very welcome.	틀림없이 대환영을 받을 것입니다.
well	[웰]	They don't speak Korean very well.	그들은 한국말을 잘하지 못해.
wide	[와이드]	How wide is the road?	길이 얼마나 넓어요?

wise
현명한
[w aiz]

wise wise wise wise

wonderful
놀라운
[w ʌ́ndərfəl]

wonderful wonderful

wrong
나쁜, 잘못된
[rɔ́ːŋ]

wrong wrong wrong

young
젊은
[jʌ́ŋ]

young young young

wise	[와이즈]	He is wise beyond all others.	그는 다른 누구보다 현명하다.
wonderful	[원더풀]	Fall is a wonderful season.	가을은 아름다운 계절이에요.
wrong	[로-ㅇ]	You've got the wrong number.	전화 잘못 거셨습니다,
young	[영]	You are too young to be in love.	사랑을 하기에는 아직 어리다

24. 부사

again
다시, 또
[əgén]

again again again again

ago
~전에
[əgóu]

ago ago ago ago ago

along
~을 따라서
[əlɔ́ːŋ]

along along along

also
역시, 또한
[ɔ́ːlsou]

also also also also also

again	[어게인]	Do it again.	다시 해 보렴.
ago	[어고우]	I met him three years ago.	3년 전에 그를 만났다.
along	[어롱]	May I come along?	따라가도 되나요?
also	[오-올쏘우]	Tom is kind, also handsome.	Tom은 착하고, 또한 잘 생겼다.

always 항상, 언제나 [ɔ́ːlwèiz]	always always	
around ~의 주위에 [əráund]	around around around	
as ~만큼 [æz]	as as as as as as as as	
away 떨어져서 [əwéi]	away away away away	
down 아래로 [daun]	down down down down	

always	[어-얼웨이즈]	Mike is always late.	Mike는 항상 늦는다.
around	[어롸운드]	I looked around the village.	저는 마을 주위를 둘러보았어요.
as	[애즈]	I will take that as a yes.	나는 승락한 것으로 알겠어요.
away	[어웨이]	Stay away from the water.	물가에 가지 마라.
down	[다운]	Turn the volume down!	볼륨을 낮춰요!

early
이른, 일찍

[ə́ːrli]

early　early　early

else
그밖에

[els]

else　else　else　else　else

even
~조차

[íːvən]

even　even　even　even

ever
이제까지

[évər]

ever　ever　ever　ever　ever

far
멀리

[faːr]

far　far　far　far　far　far

---

early	[어-ㄹ리]	I get up early in the morning.	나는 아침 일찍 일어나요.
else	[엘스]	"Anything else?"	그 밖의 다른 것은요?
even	[이-븐]	It is hot even at night.	심지어 밤에도 덥습니다.
ever	[에벌]	"Have you ever heard the song?"	그 노래 들어봤니?
far	[파-ㄹ]	The office is not far from here.	사무실은 여기서 멀지 않다

here
여기에
[hiə*r*]

here here here here

how
어떻게, 얼마나
[hau]

how how how how how

just
방금, 오직
[dʒʌst]

just just just just just

maybe
아마, 어쩌면
[méibi]

maybe maybe maybe

most
가장, 큰, 대단히
[moust]

most most most most

here	[히얼]	Bring it here at once.	그것을 당장 이리 가져오너라
how	[하우]	How are you today?	오늘은 어떻게 지냈니?
just	[줘스트]	I just arrived here.	저는 방금 여기에 도착했어요.
maybe	[메이비-]	Maybe one can help you.	도와줄 수 있을 거예요
most	[모우스트]	We have the most fun on Sundays.	일요일이 가장 즐겁다.

never
결코 ~하지 않다
[né vər]

never   never   never

no
아니, 아니오
[nou]

no no no no no no

not
아니다, 않다
[nat]

not not not not not not

now
지금, 방금
[nau]

now now now now

off
~떨어져
[ɔːf]

off off off off off

never	[네버-]	I'll never forget your kindness.
no	[노우]	No, it is not!
not	[낫]	Is it a cat? No, It is not.
now	[나우]	It is over now.
off	[어프]	Don't take off your shoes.

친절은 결코 잊지 않겠습니다
그렇지 않아요!
그것은 고양이입니다? 그것은 고양이가 아닙니다.
이제 끝났다.
신발 벗지 마세요.

174

often
자주
[ɔ́ːfən]

often often often

once
한번
[wʌns]

once once once once

out
밖에
[aut]

out out out out out out

perhaps
아마
[pərhǽps]

perhaps perhaps perhaps

quickly
빨리
[kwíkli]

quickly quickly quickly

often	[어픈]	Don't eat salt too often!	소금을 너무 자주 먹지 마세요!
once	[원스]	I have seen him once.	그와는 한 번 만난 일이 있었다.
out	[아웃]	Please get out of my room.	내 방에서 나가줘.
perhaps	[퍼햅스]	Perhaps he was lucky.	아마도 그는 운이 좋았을 것이다.
quickly	[퀵크리]	Time goes by very quickly.	시간은 매우 빨리 지나갑니다.

quite
완전히, 아주
[kwait]

quite quite quite quite

really
참으로
[ríːəli]

really really really really

slowly
천천히
[slóuli]

slowly slowly slowly

so
정말로, 그렇게
[sou]

so so so so so so so so

soon
곧
[suːn]

soon soon soon soon

---

quite	[콰이트]	It's quite obvious.	그것은 아주 명백하다
really	[리-얼리]	It was really hot last week.	지난 주는 정말 더웠습니다.
slowly	[슬로우리]	Slowly get up, get dressed.	천천히 일어나서 옷을 입으시오
so	[쏘우]	You must not behave so.	그렇게 행동해서는 안된다.
soon	[쑤-운]	See you soon.	곧 보자!

still
아직도
[stil]

still still still still still still

suddenly
갑자기
[sʌ́dnli]

suddenly suddenly

then
그 때, 그러면
[ðen]

then then then then then

there
거기에
[ðɛr]

there there there there

too
~도 또한
[tuː]

too too too too too

still	[스틸]	I'm still living in Seoul.	나는 아직 서울에 살고 있다
suddenly	[써든리]	He began to cry suddenly.	그는 갑자기 울기 시작했다.
then	[덴]	Father was a little child then.	그 당시 아버지는 작은 어린아이였다.
there	[데어]	He told me not to go there.	거기에 가지 말라고 그가 말했다
too	[튜-]	Me, too.	나 또한 그래.

twice 두번 [twais]	twice twice twice twice
up 위로 [ʌp]	up up up up up up
usually 보통 [júːʒuəli]	usually usually usually
very 매우, 아주 [véri]	very very very
well 만족하게, 잘 [wel]	well well well well

twice	[트와이스]	He is twice as old as she is.	그는 그녀보다 나이가 2배 많다.
up	[업]	Look up in the night sky.	밤 하늘을 올려다 보세요.
usually	[유-절리]	We usually eat dinner at 7 p.m.	우리는 보통 7시에 저녁을 먹는다
very	[붸뤼]	I like it very much.	난 그것을 매우 좋아해요.
well	[웰]	He speaks English very well.	그는 영어를 아주 잘한다.

when 언제 [*hw* ən]	when when when when		
where 어디에 [*hw* ɛər]	where where where		
why 왜 [*hw* ai]	why why why why		
yes 네 [jes]	yes yes yes yes yes yes		
yet 아직 [yet]	yet yet yet yet		

when	[웬]	When are you staying till?	언제까지 머물겁니까
where	[웨어]	Where did you go?	어디에 다녀왔나요?
why	[와이]	Why did they do that?	그들은 왜 그렇게 했을까요?
yes	[예스]	Yes, that's a great idea!	그거 좋은 생각이야!
yet	[예트]	We haven't eaten yet.	우리는 아직 식사를 하지 않았다

25. 전치사

about
약, 거의
[əbáut]

about about about about

above
~의 위에
[əbʌ́v]

above above above

across
~의 건너편
[əkrɔ́ːs]

across across across

after
~후에
[ǽftər]

after after after

about [어바웃]	What is the book about?	이 책은 무엇에 관한 내용이야?
above [어버브]	We see the stars above us.	우리는 머리 위의 별들을 본다.
across [어크뤄-스]	My house is across from the park.	우리집은 공원 건너편에 있어요.
after [애프터ㄹ]	Please repeat after me.	제가 말한 후에 따라하세요(제 말을 따라하세요).

along

~따라서

[əlɔ́:ŋ]

along along along along

among

~의 사이에

[əmʌ́ŋ]

among among among

at

~에서

[æt]

at at at at at at

before

~의 앞에

[bifɔ́:r]

before before before

below

~보다 아래에

[bilóu]

below below below

along	[얼러엉]	Amy walked along the street.	Amy는 길을 따라 걸었다.
among	[어멍]	The car is among the trees.	차가 나무들 사이에 있다.
at	[앳]	I study at home.	나는 집에서 공부한다.
before	[비포-르]	I read a book before I go to bed.	잠자기 전에 책을 읽습니다
below	[빌로우]	Cat is below the table.	탁자 아래 고양이가 있어요.

beside

~의 곁에

[bisáid]

beside   beside   beside

between

~의 사이에

[bitwíːn]

between   between

by

곁에, ~로써

[bai]

by   by   by   by   by   by

for

~을 위해서

[fɔːr]

for   for   for   for   for   for

from

~에서

[frʌm]

from   from   from   from   from

beside	[비싸이드]	Tom is standing beside his friends.	Tom은 친구들 옆에 서 있다.
between	[비트윈]	What happened between you two?	너희 둘 사이에 무슨 일이 있는 거야?
by	[바이]	I go to school by bus.	나는 버스 타고(버스로) 학교 가요.
for	[포-르]	This is for you.	이것은 너를 위한 거야.
from	[프럼]	I'm from Japan.	저는 일본에서 왔어요.

in	in in in in in in

in
~안에
[in]

into
~의 안으로
[ìntu]

of
~에서
[əv]

on
~의 위에
[ən]

over
~의 위에
[óuvər]

Practice: in, into, of, on, over

in	[인]	He lived in Chicago.	그는 시카고에 살았다
into	[인투]	He walked into the room.	이건 제 그는 방에 들어갔다.
of	[업]	Which of these do you want?	이것들 중에서 어느 것을 원하니?
on	[언]	The box is on the chair.	그 상자는 의자 위에 있다
over	[오우버]	The water is over his knees.	물은 그의 무릎 위까지 차 있다.

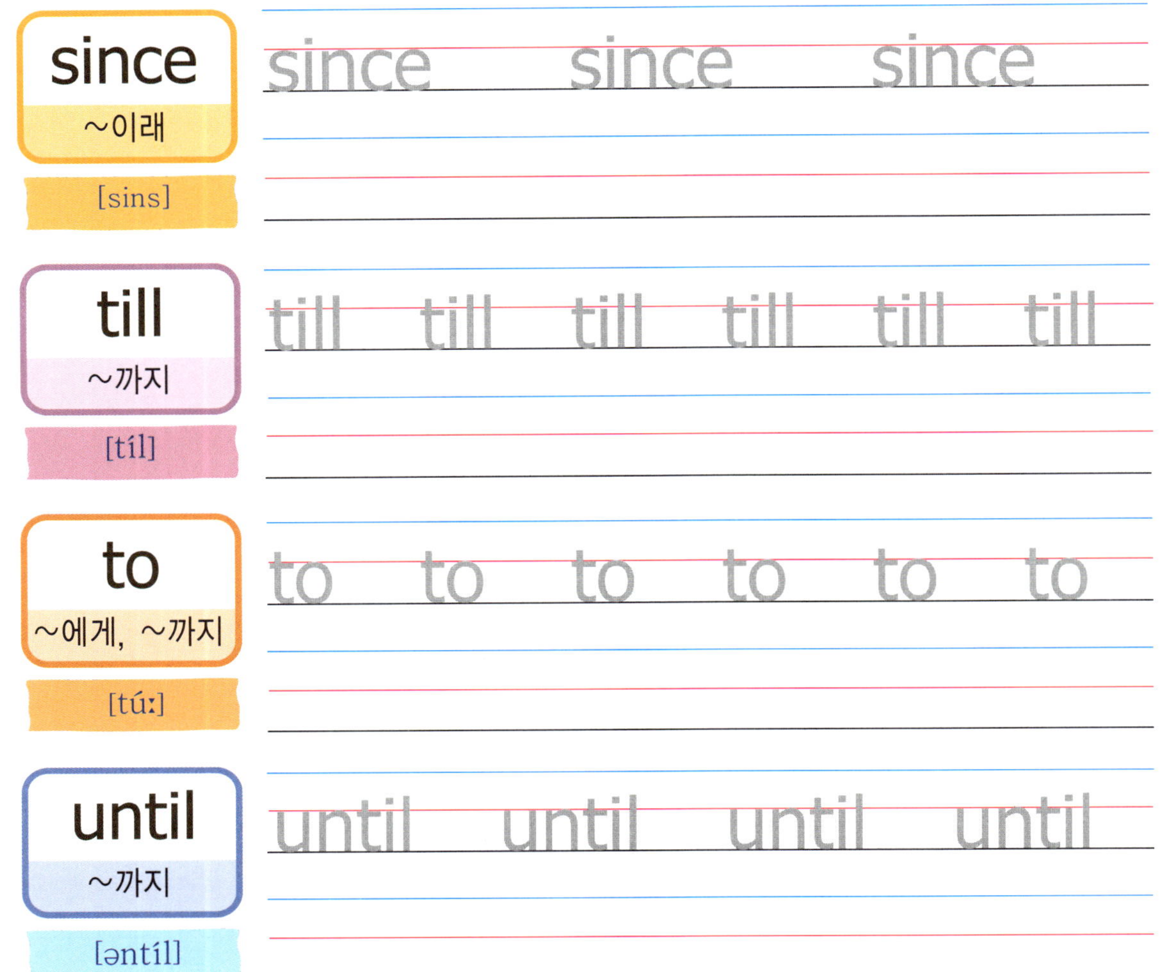

since	[씬스]	I have been here sins Ten of.	나는 10분 전부터 와 있었어요.
till	[틸]	When are you staying till?	언제까지 머물겁니까?
to	[투-]	We sailed to Europe.	배로 유럽까지 갔다
until	[언틸]	I often work until very late.	저는 종종 매우 늦게까지 일을 합니다.

26. 접속사

and
그리고, ~와
[ænd]

and　　and　　and　　and

because
왜냐하면
[bikɔ́ːz]

because　　　　because

before
~하기 전에
[bifɔ́ːr]

before　　before　　before

but
그러나, 하지만
[bʌt]

but　but　but　but　but

and	[앤드]	I like hamburger and pizza.	나는 햄버거와 피자를 좋아해.
because	[비커-즈]	I like Tom because he is kind.	나는 Tom이 좋아요. 왜냐하면 친절하니까요.
before	[비포-]	I think I have met you before.	전에 당신을 만난 적이 있는 것 같다.
but	[벗]	He likes apples. But I don't.	그는 사과를 좋아해요. 그러나 저는 안 좋아해요.

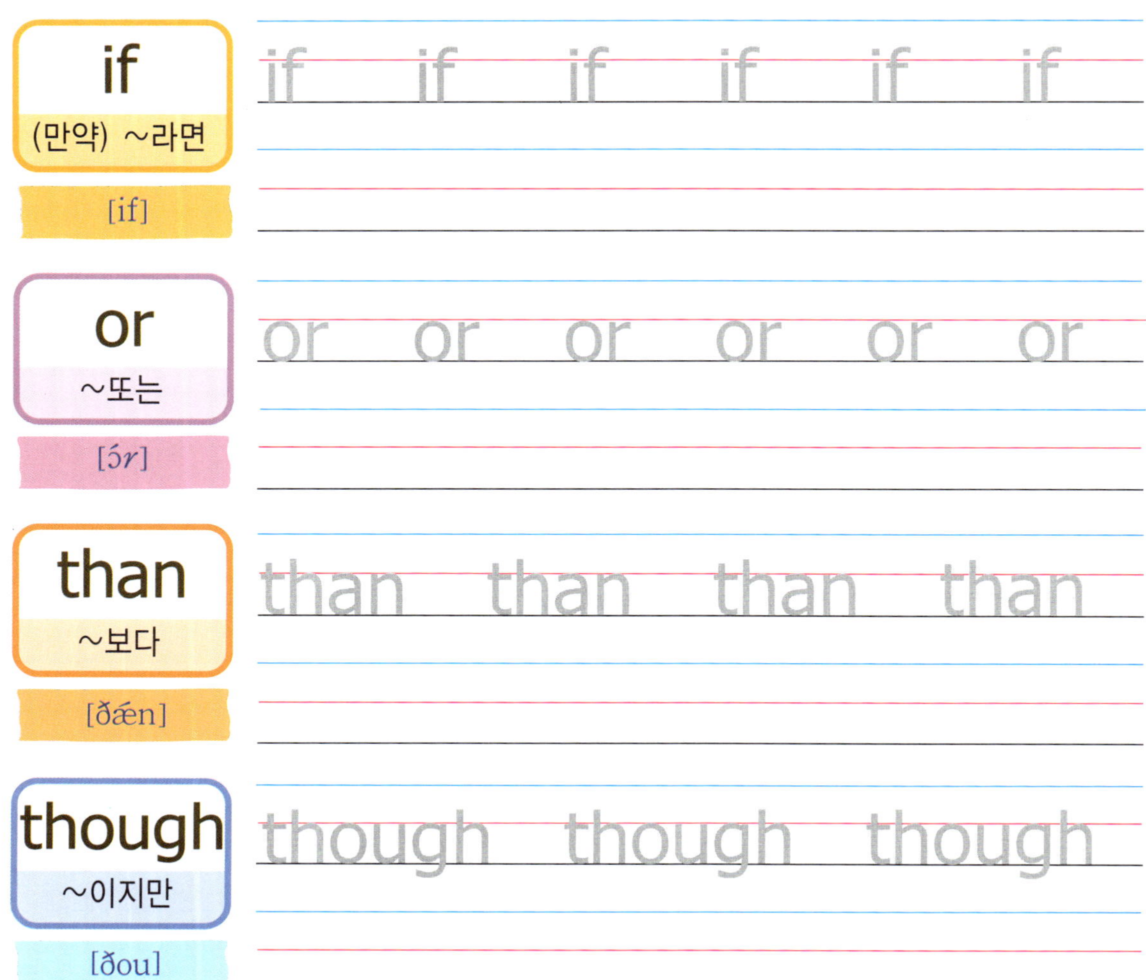

if (만약) ~라면 [if]	if if if if if if	
or ~또는 [ɔ́r]	or or or or or or	
than ~보다 [ðǽn]	than than than than	
though ~이지만 [ðou]	though though though	

if	[이프]	If I were you, I would do my best.	(만약)내가 너라면, 난 최선을 다할텐데.
or	[오-르]	Rain or shine, I'll go.	비가 오건 개건, 나는 가겠다.
than	[댄]	It is a lot bigger than Korea.	그것은 대한민국보다 훨씬 더 크다.
though	[도우]	Though he is timid, he is no coward.	그는 소심하지만 겁쟁이는 아니다.

 # 찾아보기

dark 어둠, 어두운 (107,154)
date 날짜(65)
daughter 딸(28)
day 낮, 하루(65)
deep 깊은(118,154)
deer 사슴(78)
design 디자인(92)
desk 책상(7)
die 죽다(125)
different 다른(117)
difficult 어려운, 곤란한 (115,155)
dinner 저녁 식사(43)
dirty 더러운, 불결한(155)
doctor 의사(39)
does do의 3인칭 단수 (126)
dog 개(78)
dollar 달러(89)
door 문(36)
down 아래로(104,171)
draw 끌다(126)
dress 의복(53)
drink 마시다(126)
dirty 더러운, 불결한(108)
drive 운전하다(126)
drop 떨어뜨리다(126)
drum 북, 드럼(93)
dry 마른(155)
duck 오리(79)

e

eagle 독수리(79)
ear 귀(31)
early 이른, 일찍 (155,172)
earth 지구, 땅(82)
east 동쪽(70)
easy 쉬운(114,155)
eat 먹다(127)
egg 달걀(44)
elder 손위의(156)
elephant 코끼리(79)
else 그밖에(172)
end 끝, 마치다(106)
enjoy 즐기다(127)
equal 같은, 동등한 (156,166)

eraser 지우개(7)
even ~조차(172)
evening 저녁(65)
ever 이제까지(172)
everyday 매일(65)
exact 흥분시키다(156)
excite 흥분시키다(127)
excuse 용서하다(127)
exercise 운동, 연습(92)
expensive 비싼(119)
eye 눈(32)

f

face 얼굴(32)
false 거짓의(107)
fall 가을(66)
family 가족(28)
famous 유명한(156)
far 멀리(108,172)
farmer 농부(39)
fast 빠른(118,156)
fat 살찐, 뚱뚱한(100,157)
father 아버지(28)
feel 느끼다(127)
ferry 유람선(98)
few 거의 없는(103,115)
field 들판(83)
fight 싸우다(128)
fill 채우다(128)
find 찾다, 발견하다(128)
fine 좋은, 훌륭한 (112,157)
finger 손가락(32)
finish 끝내다, 마치다(128)
fire station 소방서(58)
fish 물고기(79)
fisherman 어부(40)
fix 수리하다(129)
flower 꽃(74)
fly 날다(129)
follow 따르다(128)
food 음식(44)
foot 발(32)
for ~을 위해서(182)
forget 잊다(129)
four 4, 4의(70)
fox 여우(79)
friend 친구(13)

from ~에서(182)
fruit 과일(49)
funny 재미있는(157)

g

game 게임·놀이(93)
grandmother 할머니(28)
garden 정원(36)
gas 가스(36)
gentle 온화한, 친절한 (157)
get 얻다(129)
girl 소녀(13)
give 주다(119,129)
glad 기쁜, 반가운 (110,157)
glass 유리, 유리컵(36)
glove 장갑(53)
go 가다(107,130)
god 하느님(14)
gold 금(83)
golf 골프(93)
grape 포도(49)
gray 회색, 회색의(62)
great 큰, 엄청난(112)
green 녹색(62)
grain 곡식(74)
grass 풀(74,83)
ground 땅, 운동장(83)
group 무리, 모임, 떼(14)
grow 자라다(130)

h

hair 머리카락, 털(32)
half 반, 2분의1(70)
hall 현관(37)
ham 햄(44)
hamburger 햄버거(44)
hand 손(33)
happen 발생하다(130)
happy 행복한(158,116)
hat 모자(53)
hate 싫어하다(114,130)
have 가지고 있다(130)
hawk 매(80)
he 그는, 그가(21)
head 머리(33)
hear 듣다(131)

heart 마음, 심장(33)
help 돕다(131)
hen 암탉(80)
her 그녀의(23)
here 여기에(173)
hers 그녀의 것(21)
herself 그녀 자신(22)
heavy 무거운(100,158)
hide 숨기다, 숨다(131)
high 높은(112,158)
hiking 하이킹/도보여행 (93)
hill 언덕(83)
him 그를, 그에게(22)
himself 그 자신, 그 스스로(22)
his 그의, 그의 것(22)
hit 때리다(131)
hold 잡다, 붙들다(131)
holiday 휴일, 공휴일(66)
home 집(37)
hope 바라다(132)
horse 말(80)
hospital 병원(58)
hot 더운, 뜨거운 (114,158)
hotel 호텔(58)
hot dog 핫도그(44)
hour 시간(71)
house 집(37)
how 어떻게, 얼마나(173)
hundred 백(100)(71)
hurry 서두르다(132)
hurt 다치게 하다(132)
husband 남편(28)

i

I 나는, 내가(20)
ice 얼음(84)
idea 생각(14)
if (만약)~라면(186)
in ~안에(108,183)
ink 잉크(8)
into ~안으로(116,183)
interesting 재미있는 (159)
is ~에 있다(132)
island 섬(84)

188

it 그것은(23)
its 그것의(23)

j

jacket 재킷(53)
jam 잼(45)
job 일, 직업(40)
join 참가하다(132)
Juice 주스(45)
jump 뛰어오르다 (133,134)
jungle 밀림, 정글(84)
just 방금, 오직(173)

k

keep 계속하다(133)
key 열쇠(37)
kick 차다(133)
kill 죽이다, 없애다(133)
king 왕(14)
kitchen 부엌(37)
knee 무릎(33)
knife 칼(38)
knock 두드리다(133)
know 알다,이해하다 (134)

l

lady 숙녀, 부인(14)
lake 호수(84)
land 땅, 육지(84)
large 큰(100,159)
last 마지막으로(159)
laugh 웃다(134)
lead 인도하다(15,134)
leaf 나뭇잎(75,85)
learn 배우다(8,134)
leave 떠나다(135)
left 왼쪽, 왼쪽의(104)
leg 다리(33)

less ~보다 적은(159)
lesson 수업(8)
let 시키다(135)
letter 편지(15)
library 도서관(8,58)
lie 눕다(135)
life 생명, 생활(15)
light 가벼운(101,159)
like 좋아하다(115,135)
lily 백합(75)
lion 사자(80)
lip 입술(34)
little 약간의(113,159)
live 살다(15,135)
long 긴(114,160)
look 보다(136)
lose 잃다(136)
lot 많음(114)
love 사랑하다(136)
low 낮은, 얕은 (113,119,160)
luck 행운(15)
lucky 행운인, 운이 좋은(160)
lunch 점심(66)

m

ma'am 아주머니(29)
mail 우편(16)
main 주요한, 주된(160)
make 만들다(136)
man 남자(16)
many 많은(102,160)
map 지도(71)
marry 결혼하다(16,136)
math 수학(8)
may ~해도 좋다(137)
maybe 아마, 어쩌면(173)
me 나를(20)
meat 고기(45)
meet 만나다(137)
melon 메론(49)
men man의 복수형(16)
middle school 중학교(9)
milk 우유(45)
million 100만(71)

mine 나의 것(20)
minute 분(71)
model 모델(40)
mom 엄마(29)
money 돈(89)
monkey 원숭이(80)
month 달(66)
more 더 많은(161)
morning 아침(66)
most 가장 많은 (161,173)
mother 어머니(29)
motorcycle 오토바이(98)
mountain 산(85)
mouse 생쥐(81)
mouth 입(34)
move 움직이다(137)
movie 영화(93)
Mrs. ~부인(여자 어른)(16)
much 많은, 다량의 (102,161)
music 음악(94)

n

narrow 좁은(113,161)
nature 자연(85)
near 가까운(109,161)
neck 목(34)
need 필요로 하다(137)
nephew 조카(29)
never 결코 ~하지 않다 (174)
night 밤(67)
no 하나도 없는(174)
north 북쪽(72)
not 아니다, 않다(174)
noon 정오 한 낮(67)
nose 코(34)
now 지금, 방금(174)
number 수, 숫자(72)
nurse 간호사(40)

o

o'clock ~시(정각)(72)

of ~에서(183)
off ~떨어져(174)
office 사무실(58)
often 자주(175)
old 늙은(105,162)
on ~의 위에(105,183)
once 한번(175)
onion 양파(50)
open 열다(110,138)
or ~또는(186)
orange 오렌지 색(62)
other 다른, 그 밖의(162)
our 우리의(24)
ours 우리의 것(25)
ourselves 우리 자신이 (25)
outside 밖에(117)
out 밖으로, 밖에 (109,175)
over ~의 위에(183)
own 자기 자신의(162)

p

page 페이지(9)
paper 종이(9)
pants 바지(53)
park 공원(59)
parent 부모님(29)
party 파티,모임(17)
pass 지나가다(138)
pay 돈을 치르다(90,138)
peace 평화(17)
peach 복숭아(50)
pear (과일)배(50)
pen 펜(9)
pencil 연필(9)
people 사람들, 국민(17)
perhaps 아마(175)
photograph 사진(94)
pick 따다(138)
picnic 소풍(17)
picture 그림(94)
pig 돼지(81)
pilot 조종사(40)
pin 핀(10)
pine 소나무(75)
pineapple 파인애플(50)
pink 분홍(62)

theirs 그들의 것(24)
them 그들을(24)
themselves 그들 자신 (26)
then 그 때, 그러면(177)
there 거기에(177)
these 이것들(26)
they 그들은(23)
thick 두꺼운(166)
thin 얇은(166)
think ~라고 생각하다(147)
thirsty 목마른(167)
this 이것(25)
those 그것들(26)
throw 던지다(147)
though ~이지만(186)
to ~에게, ~까지(184)
today 오늘(68)
tomato 토마토(51)
tomorrow 내일(68)
tonight 오늘 밤(68)
too ~도 또한(177)
tooth 이, 치아(34)
touch ~을 만지다(148)
town 마을(18)
train 기차(99)
thick 두꺼운(101)
thin 얇은(100,101)
travel 여행, 여행하다(19)
trip 여행(19)
truck 트럭(99)
true 진실의(106,167)
tulip 튤립(76)
twice 두번(178)

u

uncle 아저씨, 삼촌(30)
under ~의 아래에(104)
understand 이해하다 (148)
unhappy 불행한(117)
until ~까지(184)
up 위쪽으로(105,178)
us 우리들을(25)
use 사용하다(148)
used 익숙한(167)
usually 보통(178)

v

vacation 방학(11)
vegetable 야채(51)
very 매우, 아주(178)
video 비디오(96)
village 마을, 촌락(19)
viine 덩굴(76)
violin 바이올린(96)
visit 방문하다(73)

w

wait 기다리다(148)
wake 깨다(148)
walk 걷다, 산책하다(149)
want 원하다(149)
warm 따뜻한(112,167)
was am,is의 과거형 (149)
water 물(87)
way 길, 방법(73)
we 우리, 저희가(24)
weak 약한(111,168)
wear 입고 있다(149)
weed 잡초(76)
week 주, 1주간(68)
weekend 주말(69)
welcome 환영하다 (19,168)
well 만족하게, 잘 (168,178)
went 갔다(149)
were are의 과거형(158)
west 서쪽(73)
wheat 밀(76)
when 언제(179)
where 어디에(179)
white 흰, 흰빛(63)
why 왜(179)
wide 넓은(112,168)
wife 부인(30)
will ~일 것이다(150)
win 이기다(150)
wind 바람(87)
winter 겨울(69)
wise 현명한(169)

woman 여자(19)
wonder 이상하게 여기 다(150)
wonderful 놀라운(169)
worst 최악의(107)
write 쓰다, 편지를 쓰다 (150)
wrong 나쁜, 잘못된 (169)

x

xylophone 실로폰 (96)

y

year 년, 나이(69)
yellow 노랑(63)
yes 예, 네(179)
yesterday 어제(69)
yet 아직(179)
you 너, 당신(21)
young 젊은, 어린 (104,169)
your 너의, 너희들의(21)
yours 너의 것(21)
yourself 너 자신, 너 스스로(24)

z

zero 0, 영(69)
zoo 동물원(81)

초등 영단어 850 따라쓰기

재판 4쇄 발행 2022년 7월 31일

글 Y&M 어학 연구소

펴낸이 서영희 | **펴낸곳** 와이 앤 엠

편집 임명아 | **책임교정** 하연정

본문인쇄 명성 인쇄 | **제책** 정화 제책

제작 이윤식 | **마케팅** 강성태

주소 120-848 서울시 서대문구 홍은동 376-28

전화 (02)308-3891 | **Fax** (02)308-3892

E-mail yam3891@naver.com

등록 2007년 8월 29일 제312-2007-000040호

ISBN 978-89-93557-44-2 63740

본사는 출판물 윤리강령을 준수합니다.